CW00502387

THE ART OF PROMPT PERFECTION:
Mastering AI Conversations

By Taha Baba

Book Blurb

"The Art of Prompt Perfection: Mastering AI Conversations" is an essential guide for anyone seeking to navigate the rapidly evolving world of Artificial Intelligence (AI) and conversational agents. In this groundbreaking book, readers will embark on a journey through the intricate realm of AI dialogues, unravelling the art and science of prompt design. This book is not just a collection of theories; it's a beacon of practical wisdom and cutting-edge research, illuminating the path for amateurs and experts alike, in the dynamic domain of AI interactions.

The story of AI has always been one of wonder and complexity, from its humble beginnings to its current status, as a transformative force in technology. This book delves deep into the evolution of AI, tracing its history and celebrating its milestones. We will demystify the complex language models that have revolutionized how we interact with machines, making them an integral part of our daily lives.

At the heart of this interaction lies the craft of prompt design; a skill, crucial, yet often overlooked. "The Art of Prompt Perfection" unravels the components of a well-designed prompt: command, context, clarity, and creativity. These elements, when skilfully woven together, unlock AI's vast potential, paving the way for meaningful and effective human-AI interactions. Through a series of rich examples and detailed case studies, we demonstrate how nuanced prompt design can dramatically alter AI responses, turning basic exchanges into rich, informative dialogues.

But our journey doesn't stop here. We will take you through the practical applications of AI across various sectors, showcasing how strategic prompt design enhances business operations, revolutionizes educational practices, and enriches personal life. We'll explore advanced prompt techniques, tailoring prompts for specific AI models, and unlocking AI's potential for creativity and innovation.

In an era where AI's impact transcends geographical and cultural boundaries, so emerges challenges and strategies of crafting prompts that respect and embrace linguistic and cultural diversity. As we peer into the future, we can analyze emerging technologies and speculate on the next generation of AI conversational agents, contemplating their potential impact on society and prompt design.

Ethical considerations are paramount in the dawning age of AI. "The Art of Prompt Perfection" addresses this critical aspect, guiding readers through the development of ethical prompts, privacy navigation, and responsible AI interactions. This book champions the importance of ethical integrity and best practices in AI usage, ensuring that advancements in technology are matched by a commitment to moral responsibility.

For enthusiasts, professionals, and curious minds, this book is a treasure trove of knowledge, offering insights and skills essential for mastering AI conversations. As AI continues to weave its way deeper into the fabric of our existence, "The Art of Prompt Perfection: Mastering AI Conversations" stands as a testament to human ingenuity and a guide to harnessing the incredible power of AI in a responsible, effective, and ethical manner. Join us on this enlightening journey to master the art of AI communication, where every prompt opens a door to endless possibilities.

Taha Baba

Taha Baba

Book Preface

Welcome to "The Art of Prompt Perfection: Mastering AI Conversations", a comprehensive guide designed to navigate the intricate and rapidly evolving world of Artificial Intelligence (AI) and its interaction with human language. This book is an amalgamation of research, practice, and visionary insights into the field of AI, particularly focusing on the crucial role of prompt design in enhancing and steering AI conversations. Our primary objective is to provide a rich, informative resource for a broad spectrum of readers – from AI enthusiasts and students to professionals and novices in the field. The vision behind this work is to demystify the complexities of AI conversations and present a clear, accessible guide to prompt designing; a pivotal yet often underexplored aspect of AI interaction. We strive to bridge the gap between theoretical AI concepts and their practical applications, ensuring that our readers gain both foundational knowledge and actionable skills.

The journey of AI has been nothing short of revolutionary. From its conceptual inception to becoming a cornerstone of modern technology, AI has continuously reshaped our interaction with the digital world. This text will traverse through this fascinating journey, highlighting significant milestones and the latest advancements in AI technology. Our exploration includes the evolution of language models, the development of conversational agents, and the impact of prompt design on AI performance. At the core of effective AI interactions lies the art of crafting precise and impactful prompts. The pages to follow delve deep into what constitutes a well-designed prompt, dissecting its essential elements - command, context, clarity, and creativity. Through various examples and real-life case studies, we demonstrate the profound influence of these components on the quality and effectiveness of AI responses. Another of the book's key focuses is on mastering the balance between clarity and creativity in prompt design. We provide a detailed overview of clear communication principles in AI, the importance of precision in prompt crafting, and strategies for navigating the spectrum of prompt specificity. This section is enriched with illustrative examples, contrasting clear versus complex prompts, and showcasing real-world applications of specific versus open prompts.

The practical applications of AI in business, education, and daily life form a significant part of our discussion. We bring forward real-life examples and case studies where AI, powered by well-designed prompts, has led to enhanced solutions and experiences. Additionally, we delve into advanced prompt techniques, focusing on tailoring prompts for specific AI models and unleashing AI's potential for creativity and innovation. In today's globalized world, the impact of cultural and linguistic diversity on prompt design is crucial. This book addresses the challenges and strategies of adapting prompts for global AI interactions, ensuring inclusivity and accuracy in multicultural AI communication. As we look towards the future, we speculate on emerging technologies in AI and their potential impact on prompt design. We discuss the role of AI interpretability in prompt crafting and ponder over the speculative futures of next-generation AI conversational agents. Ethical considerations and best practices form the bedrock of our discussion, emphasizing responsible AI interaction and the development of ethical prompts.

"The Art of Prompt Perfection: Mastering AI Conversations" is not just a book; it's a journey into the heart of AI communication. It's an invitation to engage with AI technology, understand its nuances, and master the skill of prompt designing to foster effective, ethical, and enriching AI interactions.

Taha Baba

Introduction to AI and Conversational Agents

Overview of AI and its Evolution

The journey of Artificial Intelligence (AI) is a chronicle of human ambition and technological triumph. From the moment the concept of artificial beings first ignited the imaginations of ancient mythmakers and storytellers, to the contemporary landscape where AI conversational agents are a reality, the evolution of AI has been nothing short of extraordinary.

A Brief History of AI

In tracing the development of AI from its inception, we observe a fascinating progression. The story begins in earnest in the mid-20th century, marked by a confluence of mathematics, logic, and burgeoning computer science. The field's patriarchs, Alan Turing, and John McCarthy, among others, laid the intellectual groundwork, proposing machines that could simulate every aspect of learning and any other feature of intelligence.

The initial forays into AI were characterized by rule-based systems, where decision-making was driven by pre-set instructions. These were the early attempts at codifying knowledge and reasoning into a language that machines could understand and execute. Despite the limitations of these systems, they were fundamental to advancing the field, leading to the development of more sophisticated algorithms.

The history of Artificial Intelligence (AI) is a tale of dreams metamorphosing into reality. It's a narrative that spans from the philosophical musings of antiquity to the advanced computational algorithms we witness today. In the following prose, we continue to explore this remarkable history, and take into account the myriad achievements that have collectively shaped the domain of AI.

AI's inception can be traced back to when humans first conceived the notion of automatons capable of mimicking human actions. However, it wasn't until the 20th century that these ideas began to crystallize into a scientific reality. The field's official birth came with the Dartmouth Conference in 1956, where the term 'Artificial Intelligence' was formally coined, marking a new epoch in technological pursuit.

Early AI research was marked by the development of systems that could perform specific tasks, a primitive form of what we would recognize today as AI. Programs like the Logic Theorist and ELIZA were groundbreaking, demonstrating that machines could undertake tasks previously thought to be the sole remit of human intellect. The ensuing decades witnessed AI's potential and limitations. The field experienced its first winters—periods of reduced funding and waning interest due to over-ambitious expectations and underwhelming results. Yet, even as public enthusiasm fluctuated, dedicated researchers persisted, laying the groundwork for future advancements.

Taha Baba

In the 1980s, a resurgence occurred with the emergence of machine learning algorithms. These algorithms allowed machines not just to 'think' but to 'learn', marking a pivotal shift from static to dynamic systems. The evolution of neural networks, particularly deep learning networks in the 2000s, revolutionized AI's capabilities, enabling machines to analyse and learn from vast amounts of data.

The turn of the millennium brought AI into the public conscience like never before. With the advent of sophisticated language models, AI began to understand and generate human language, leading to the development of conversational agents. These agents could engage with humans in natural dialogue, learning from each interaction and becoming increasingly sophisticated over time.

As we advanced into the 21st century, AI became ubiquitous. From autonomous vehicles to intelligent personal assistants, AI systems are now integral to many aspects of our daily lives. The design of AI prompts, which guide these interactions, has become a specialized field of study, reflecting the importance of effective communication in the utilization of AI technologies.

The history of AI is a continuum, marked by periods of both fervent excitement and cautious scepticism. It's a field defined by its relentless pursuit of innovation—a pursuit that continues to push the boundaries of what's possible. As we press forward, the promise of AI looms ever larger. The future holds the potential for AI that can better understand and interact with the world, blurring the lines between human and machine intelligence.

The next chapters of AI's history will be shaped by advances in quantum computing, ethical AI frameworks, and machines that may one day express emotions indistinguishable from our own. The narrative of AI is far from complete, and the chapters that remain unwritten are as exciting as those that have passed. As we look to the future, we carry the lessons of history with us, knowing that each new discovery stands upon the shoulders of what came before. Our journey through the annals of AI's past is a foundational step in mastering the art of prompt perfection in AI conversations.

Milestones in AI Evolution

The first milestone came with the realization that for AI to truly emulate human intelligence, it had to learn from experience. This gave rise to machine learning, a subfield of AI that focuses on the development of systems that can learn from and make decisions based on data. Machine learning's ascendance in the AI hierarchy was bolstered by the emergence of neural networks, which sought to mimic the neural structures of the human brain.

As the digital era surged forward, the availability of vast amounts of data and the computational power to process it led to the development of deep learning. This marked a significant turning point, birthing systems capable of image and speech recognition—tasks that were previously deemed too complex for machines.

Within the chronicles of AI, certain milestones stand out, representing significant leaps in the field's evolution. These accomplishments have not only shaped the trajectory of AI but have also set the stage for the advanced AI conversations and prompt designs that we interact with today.

The earliest milestones were conceptual, born from intellectual curiosity and theoretical work. In the 1950s, the Turing Test, proposed by Alan Turing, became one of the first formal challenges that sought to measure a machine's ability to exhibit intelligent behaviour indistinguishable from that of a human. This challenge laid the groundwork for future explorations into AI.

As AI research gained momentum, the 1960s and 1970s saw the creation of the first problem-solving programs. These included the General Problem Solver and DENDRAL, which marked AI's nascent ability to process complex information and make decisions. Yet, these were constrained by their rule-based nature and lack of learning capability.

The next leap forward came with the development of machine learning in the 1980s, where AI systems were designed to learn from data. This was a paradigm shift, as it moved AI from static to dynamic, adaptive systems. The introduction of the backpropagation algorithm revolutionized neural networks, enhancing their learning capabilities.

The 1990s witnessed the emergence of the internet and the digital explosion, which provided unprecedented amounts of data. This data became the fuel for machine learning algorithms, leading to improved natural language processing and the first interactive conversational agents.

Entering the 21st century, AI milestones became increasingly practical and integrated into everyday life. The development of IBM's Watson, which triumphed in the game show 'Jeopardy!', demonstrated AI's ability to understand and process natural language at a high level. Similarly, the victory of Google's AlphaGo over the world champion in the game of Go marked a significant achievement in strategic AI decision-making.

Simultaneously, advancements in deep learning enabled the creation of AI systems with capabilities that were once the domain of science fiction. These systems began to drive cars, create art, and write texts, showcasing the versatility and potential of AI. One of the most pivotal recent highlights is the development of transformer-based language models like OpenAI's GPT-3. These models represent a quantum leap in AI's ability to generate coherent and contextually relevant text, making conversational agents more nuanced and responsive than ever before.

Each of these discoveries, has contributed to the art and science of prompt design. They have informed the strategies used to communicate with AI, shaping the prompts to be more effective and intuitive. This has resulted in conversational agents that can engage in more complex dialogues, understand a wider range of queries, and provide more accurate and helpful responses.

As we dive deeper into the "The Art of Prompt Perfection: Mastering AI Conversations", we will explore how these milestones have directly influenced the development of AI prompt design. We will examine the intersection of AI advancements with practical applications, ethical considerations, and future trends. The history of AI is not just a story of technological progress; it is also a narrative of human ingenuity and creativity, which continues to evolve and inspire the field of AI conversations.

Taha Baba

The Evolution of Language Models

With the progression of machine learning and deep learning, natural language processing took a significant leap forward. The evolution of language models has been instrumental in the rise of conversational agents. These models have allowed machines to parse, understand, and generate human language with increasing sophistication, enabling seamless and natural communication with users.

The history of language models in AI is a compelling saga of innovation, mirroring the quest to bridge human and machine communication. As a pivotal element in the tapestry of AI development, language models have undergone a remarkable transformation, evolving from simple pattern-recognition systems to intricate models that can emulate nuanced human dialogue.

The origins of language models in AI can be traced back to the early days of computer science, where the first attempts to process natural language were rooted in rule-based systems. These systems operated on fixed algorithms that could interpret and generate language based on a predefined set of rules. However, their rigidity and limited scope soon gave way to more sophisticated approaches.

The shift from rule-based to statistical language models marked a significant advancement. This change leveraged the power of probability to predict word sequences, leading to more flexible and accurate language processing. Statistical models, such as Hidden Markov Models and n-gram models, paved the way for the early stages of machine translation and speech recognition, setting a new standard in AI's linguistic capabilities.

The advent of machine learning, especially deep learning, revolutionized language models. Neural networks, with their ability to learn representations of data, brought about the era of embedding models. These models captured semantic relationships between words, resulting in language processing that was contextually aware and semantically rich. They were instrumental in the development of sentiment analysis, language generation, and more sophisticated conversational agents.

The true game-changer in the domain of language models was the introduction of sequence-to-sequence models, which allowed for end-to-end training on language tasks. This breakthrough was particularly transformative for translation services, enabling more accurate and fluid translations than ever before. However, the landscape of language models was forever altered with the creation of transformer models, like OpenAI's GPT series and Google's BERT.

These models abandoned the sequential processing of language for a parallel approach, dramatically improving the efficiency and effectiveness of language understanding and generation. With these models, AI began to master a wide array of linguistic tasks, from summarization to question-answering, with an unprecedented level of proficiency.

Transformers also marked the beginning of AI systems that could generate human-like text, allowing for the creation of prompts that were conversational, contextually relevant, and capable of sustaining dialogue. The implications for conversational agents were profound, as they could now understand and respond to a wider range of human input with greater accuracy and relevance.

As we explore the future of language models, we stand on the cusp of breakthroughs that could redefine human-AI interaction. From models that can understand the subtleties of tone and emotion to those that

Taha Baba

can engage in complex reasoning, the potential for more advanced and empathetic conversational agents is immense.

In the continuum of AI's linguistic evolution, the next frontier lies in models that can learn from less data, understand more languages, and engage in more meaningful and creative conversations. The journey of language models is far from over, and its trajectory suggests a future where AI may not only understand all human languages, but also create new ones, fostering an era of unprecedented interconnectivity and understanding.

The evolution of language models encapsulates the essence of AI's broader evolution—a testament to human ingenuity and the relentless pursuit of machines that can converse, comprehend, and connect in the most human of ways. As we delve deeper into the world of AI conversations and prompt design, these language models stand as both the foundation and the beacon for what AI can and will achieve.

Defining Conversational Agents

Conversational agents, born from the union of AI and language models, are now prevalent across various platforms. They range from text-based chatbots that provide customer service to voice-activated assistants that manage our homes and daily schedules. These agents are the embodiment of AI's conversational capabilities and a testament to the power of prompt design in shaping their interactions.

The narrative of AI's evolution is ongoing and vibrant, with each chapter adding depth and dimension to the way we interact with technology. As we continue to develop and refine AI, it is clear that our communication with these systems, through the design of effective prompts, remains at the heart of AI's potential to transform our world.

In the grand narrative of Artificial Intelligence, conversational agents represent a synthesis of technological prowess and the innate human desire for connection. These agents, often the most visible and interactive embodiments of AI, are systems designed to communicate with humans through language that is natural and intuitive. They are not merely tools but companions and helpers, growing ever more sophisticated with each advancement in AI.

Conversational agents, also known as chatbots or virtual assistants, have risen from the realm of simple scripted interactions to becoming complex entities capable of learning, adapting, and providing personalized experiences. Their defining characteristic lies in their ability to engage in dialogue that is not only coherent but contextually aware and responsive to the nuances of human communication.

The importance of conversational agents in today's digital landscape cannot be overstated. They serve as the frontline of customer service for many organizations, handling inquiries, solving problems, and providing support around the clock. Beyond customer service, these agents facilitate a myriad of tasks, from teaching languages to providing therapy and companionship.

In the commercial sphere, conversational agents drive engagement by offering users a seamless way to interact with services and products. In the home, they help manage tasks and control smart devices, becoming an integral part of daily life. In education, they personalize learning, adapting content to suit

Taha Baba

the learner's pace and style. Their versatility is a testament to their design, which combines the fields of computational linguistics, psychology, and computer science.

The evolution of conversational agents is closely linked to the evolution of language models in AI. Early conversational agents were limited by the scope of their programming, able to respond only to a narrow set of inputs. However, as language models have grown more advanced, so too have the capabilities of these agents. Today's agents can handle a broad range of topics and maintain context over the course of a conversation, providing responses that are increasingly indistinguishable from a human interlocutor.

Yet, defining conversational agents is not just a matter of outlining their functions; it is also about understanding their significance in a world where the lines between human and machine are blurring. These agents represent a step towards a future where AI not only understands our words but also grasps our intentions, emotions, and desires. They are at the forefront of a shift in how we interact with technology, transforming it from a passive tool to an active participant in our lives.

The impact of conversational agents on society and industry is profound. They have the potential to revolutionize customer service, education, and personal assistance. They challenge us to rethink the nature of work, the structure of our days, and the manner in which we communicate. They also raise important questions about privacy, security, and the ethics of AI—questions that must be addressed as these agents become more ingrained in our lives.

As we continue to develop and refine these agents, we must do so with a sense of responsibility and foresight. Conversational agents are not just a reflection of AI's capabilities but also of our values, our culture, and our collective vision for the future. They are a bridge between us and the ever-expanding possibilities of artificial intelligence—a bridge that we are still in the process of building.

The Importance of Conversational Agents

Conversational agents stand as modern-day avatars of AI, bridging the once yawning chasm between human complexity and computational simplicity. Their significance transcends the bounds of mere convenience, touching upon the very fabric of societal interaction and digital communication.

These agents, crafted from lines of code and machine learning algorithms, are the manifestations of a world increasingly inclined towards digital interconnectivity. They are not only facilitators of task execution but also pioneers in the field of AI, exemplifying how technology can emulate the intricacies of human conversation. By simulating the nuances of human dialogue, they serve as a testament to the astonishing leaps AI has made in understanding and generating natural language.

The role of conversational agents is multifaceted. In business, they have transformed customer service, providing support and assistance with unprecedented efficiency. The advent of AI-driven chatbots has enabled companies to engage with customers instantaneously, addressing their queries and concerns around the clock, without the need for human intervention. This revolution has not only optimized customer experiences, but also allowed businesses to allocate human resources to more complex tasks that require emotional intelligence and nuanced judgment.

Taha Baba

In the realm of personal assistance, conversational agents like Siri, Alexa, and Google Assistant have become household names, orchestrating the rhythms of daily life with an ever-expanding repertoire of skills. They control our devices, manage our schedules, and even entertain us, becoming integral to the smart home ecosystem. Their constant evolution reflects a relentless pursuit of greater contextual awareness and personalized interaction, two hallmarks of human-like communication.

Moreover, these agents are crucial in the democratization of information access. They break down barriers for those who may struggle with traditional computing interfaces, such as the elderly or differently-abled, by providing a more natural and intuitive mode of interaction—spoken or typed language. In this way, they embody the principles of inclusive design and accessibility, ensuring that the benefits of technology can be enjoyed by a broader segment of society.

The impact of conversational agents also extends to the domain of education, where they offer personalized learning experiences. As AI tutors, they adapt to individual learning styles and paces, providing educational content that is tailored to the learner's needs. This adaptive learning approach promises to reshape the educational landscape, making learning more accessible, engaging, and effective for students worldwide.

As we continue to explore the symbiotic relationship between humans and machines, conversational agents represent a critical juncture in this journey. They challenge us to refine our understanding of AI, pushing the boundaries of what it means to communicate and connect. Their development and widespread adoption herald a new era where AI is not a mere tool but a companion and collaborator in the human story.

In the broader context, conversational agents underscore the importance of ethical AI development. As these entities become more ingrained in our lives, it is imperative that they are designed with a keen awareness of privacy, security, and ethical considerations. They must be built to respect user data, provide transparent interactions, and avoid reinforcing societal biases.

Conversational agents are more than a technological marvel; they are a beacon of the AI renaissance, a focal point where human desires for interaction, efficiency, and assistance converge with the capabilities of artificial intelligence. Their evolution is a reflection of our own, growing more sophisticated, more connected, and more integral to the tapestry of human life with each passing day.

Different Types of Conversational Agents

Conversational agents are the progeny of artificial intelligence, designed to converse with humans in a way that mimics our own patterns of communication. These digital interlocutors come in various forms, each tailored to specific tasks and interactions. Their diversity is not merely technical but also functional, ranging from simplistic scripted bots to complex AI that can engage in seemingly natural and spontaneous dialogue.

Taha Baba

Scripted Chatbots

At the most basic level, scripted chatbots operate on predefined rules. They are the stalwarts of online customer service, programmed to respond to specific inputs with specific outputs. Their intelligence is not in their ability to understand, but rather in their capacity to recognize keywords and retrieve information accordingly. They are fast, efficient, and often the first point of contact between businesses and customers online, handling straightforward queries with ease.

Interactive Voice Response (IVR) Systems

IVR systems are conversational agents that interact via voice instead of text. They are often employed in call centres to direct callers to the appropriate department or provide automated responses to common inquiries. Although their interaction is based on a set of predetermined options, advances in natural language processing (NLP) have allowed for more sophisticated and less rigid IVR systems that can understand and process more natural speech patterns.

Intelligent Virtual Assistants

Intelligent virtual assistants, such as Siri, Alexa, and Google Assistant, are the household names of conversational agents. They utilize advanced NLP and machine learning to perform a wide range of tasks. From setting alarms to offering weather updates and controlling smart home devices, these assistants learn from each interaction, gradually personalizing their responses to the user's preferences and patterns.

AI Tutors and Coaches

In the educational domain, AI tutors and coaching systems provide personalized learning experiences. They can adapt in real-time to the learner's pace, offer explanations, and guide through complex concepts. By leveraging machine learning, they can identify patterns in a student's learning process and tailor their instructional approach accordingly.

Therapeutic Chatbots

Emerging at the intersection of technology and mental health, therapeutic chatbots offer conversational support to users seeking psychological assistance. They employ empathetic listening and provide responses that mimic a therapeutic conversation, offering comfort and guidance. While not replacements for professional care, they extend a line of first response to those who may not have immediate access to human therapists.

Multilingual Conversational Agents

Multilingual conversational agents break down language barriers, offering real-time translation and facilitating cross-cultural communication. They recognize and process multiple languages, allowing for

Taha Baba

seamless dialogue between speakers of different tongues. Their sophistication lies in their ability to understand context, idioms, and cultural nuances, which are essential for accurate translation.

Domain-Specific Agents

These agents are experts in a specific field, be it legal, medical, or financial. They understand jargon and can provide specialized information or assistance. Their training involves deep learning within a particular knowledge base, allowing them to handle complex queries that require expertise.

Autonomous Agents for Gaming and Simulation

In the world of gaming and simulations, autonomous conversational agents provide dynamic interactions, adapting to the player's actions and contributing to a more immersive experience. They can role-play, assist, or challenge players, driven by AI that enables them to respond unpredictably and engagingly.

The ecosystem of conversational agents is rich and varied, with each type serving unique purposes and challenges. Their development reflects the advances in AI and machine learning, showcasing the potential for machines to engage with us in increasingly sophisticated and helpful ways. As AI continues to evolve, so too will the capabilities and variety of these conversational agents, promising new levels of interactivity and assistance in our digital lives.

The Impact of Prompt Design on AI Performance

The potency of a conversational AI's performance is tightly woven into the fabric of its prompt design. This is not merely a matter of software engineering but of linguistic finesse and psychological insight. Prompt design is the crucible in which the effectiveness of AI interactions is forged, with each phrase and word choice serving as a variable in the complex equation of human-AI communication.

Clarity in prompt design propels AI towards relevance and precision. Clear prompts cut through the potential fog of miscommunication, providing AI with an unambiguous directive to follow. This is especially crucial in domains where specificity is paramount, such as technical support or medical diagnosis, where the cost of misunderstanding could be high.

Context as the Compass

Context in a prompt serves as a compass for AI, orienting it not just to the immediate request but to the broader situation at hand. It is context that enables an AI to discern whether a reference to "Apple" is seeking information on fruit, technology, or even stocks. Embedding context within prompts is akin to providing a map to the AI unit, guiding it to the destination of a relevant response.

The Dance of Specificity and Flexibility

Taha Baba

Effective prompts strike a delicate balance between specificity and flexibility. Too specific, and the AI's responses may become rigid and myopic. Too broad, and its responses may drift into the irrelevant. The art lies in crafting prompts that are precise enough to be clear but flexible enough to allow for the AI's computational creativity to shine through.

Creativity within Constraints

In the realm of creative tasks, the design of prompts must leave room for AI to manoeuvre and innovate. A prompt asking for a story about a journey can take on infinite forms, and it is the subtle nudges within the prompt that can inspire an AI to generate a tale of epic adventure or quiet introspection.

Prompting for Personalization

The evolution of AI has brought personalization to the forefront, and prompt design has had to adapt accordingly. Personalized prompts use data and insights from previous interactions to tailor responses to the individual, enhancing user satisfaction and engagement. For example, a prompt for music recommendations would benefit from knowing the user's past preferences and listening habits.

Training AI with Thoughtful Prompts

Behind every conversational AI lies a training process shaped by the prompts it has been fed. Thoughtfully designed prompts used in training set the stage for competent AI, capable of engaging in nuanced and meaningful dialogue. It is through this careful training that AI begins to approximate the complexities of human conversation.

Measuring the Impact of Prompts

The real-world impact of prompt design on AI performance can be measured through user satisfaction, task completion rates, and the AI's ability to engage in prolonged and coherent dialogues. A/B testing different prompt designs can yield insights into the most effective strategies, allowing developers to fine-tune their approach.

To sum up, the design of prompts is a pivotal factor in determining the performance of conversational AI. It is a multidisciplinary endeavour that blends language arts, cognitive science, and computer programming. As AI continues to integrate into every aspect of our digital lives, the importance of prompt design only grows, making it a field ripe for innovation and requiring a deep understanding of both the technology and the human psyche it seeks to emulate. Through meticulous prompt design, we unlock the full potential of AI as a partner in conversation, an aid in tasks, and a gateway to new realms of digital interaction.

Taha Baba

The Anatomy of a Prompt

Understanding the Core Elements

When engaging with artificial intelligence, the prompt stands as the pivotal interface through which human intention is translated into digital understanding. It is the bridge between two worlds, marrying human thought with machine processing. Grasping the anatomy of a prompt is much like learning a new language—a language that AI not only understands but responds to with precision and relevance.

The importance of this understanding cannot be understated. In the realm of AI, a well-crafted prompt is a powerful tool. It has the potential to unlock the vast capabilities of AI, turning a simple question into a gateway for knowledge, a directive into an action, and a creative spark into a masterpiece. Crafting an effective AI prompt is akin to composing a symphony, where each element plays a vital role in its overall performance.

An effective prompt is the heart of AI communication. Just as a heart pumps blood to all parts of the body, a prompt circulates the intent and purpose throughout the AI system, enabling it to function and interact effectively. Without a robust understanding of prompt anatomy, one might struggle to harness the full potential of AI, much like a musician attempting to play a composition without understanding the nuances of their instrument.

Therefore, dissecting the anatomy of a prompt is crucial for anyone looking to master AI conversations. It equips individuals with the knowledge to craft prompts that are not only understood by AI but also elicit the most coherent, contextual, and useful responses. Whether it's simplifying a complex problem, seeking an inventive solution, or just navigating the digital space, understanding the anatomy of a prompt is the first step towards fluency in the language of AI.

Let us explore these core elements briefly, as each will be dissected in detail in their respective sections to follow.

Command

The Directive Force In AI Interactions

The command is the crux of a prompt, acting as the directive force that compels the AI to take action. It is an essential element, serving as a beacon that guides the AI through the vast sea of data and possibilities to arrive at the intended destination. Understanding the nature and power of commands is critical for anyone looking to craft effective AI prompts.

At its core, a command in the context of AI prompt design is an instruction that is explicitly stated to provoke a response or action from the AI system. It is the element that gives the prompt a purpose,

Taha Baba

whether it's retrieving information, performing a task, or creating content. Commands are the first point of interaction, the questions we pose, the tasks we assign, and the creativity we seek to invoke from AI.

Crafting Clear Commands

Creating clear commands is an art that balances brevity with detail. It involves being concise enough to be understood by the AI, yet detailed enough to avoid ambiguity. A clear command eliminates confusion and ensures that the AI's response is aligned with the user's expectations. It is the difference between a command that reads "Give me weather" — which is vague and open-ended — and one that specifies "What is the weather forecast for Paris tomorrow?" — which directs the AI to provide a specific piece of information.

Command in Context

The command does not exist in a vacuum; it is often framed within a context that enhances its meaning and shapes the AI's response. For instance, the command "Play some music" takes on different meanings when paired with "Play some music from the 80s" versus "Play some relaxing music for meditation". The context here fine-tunes the command, instructing the AI to filter its vast musical repertoire to match the user's mood or preference.

The Role of Command in User Experience

The effectiveness of a command also has a significant impact on the user experience. A well-phrased command leads to a satisfying interaction, where the AI meets the user's needs efficiently. Conversely, a poorly structured command can result in frustration and a breakdown in communication. Therefore, understanding the subtleties of command formulation is key to enhancing the user experience in AI interactions.

The Power of Command

The command is the starting line of the AI conversation race. It sets the pace, direction, and the parameters of the interaction. Mastering the use of commands in prompt design is thus essential for harnessing the full capabilities of AI, ensuring that each interaction is a step towards achieving the precise outcomes desired by the user. As we continue to explore the anatomy of a prompt, the significance of the command as the initial, directing force will be echoed in every aspect of AI interaction, underpinning the power of effective communication in the digital realm.

Context

Shaping AI Understanding and Responses

Taha Baba

In the anatomy of a prompt, context acts as the scaffolding that shapes the AI's understanding and response. It is the background information, the setting, the backstory that informs the AI of the where, when, who, and why of a command, enabling it to generate a response that is not only accurate but also situationally appropriate.

The context is a multifaceted concept in prompt design. It encompasses everything from the user's historical interactions with the AI to the environmental variables that could affect the response. A command without context is like a traveller without a map; it may eventually reach a destination, but the journey is likely to be inefficient and fraught with missteps.

Embedding Context in AI Prompts

Embedding context in AI prompts is a delicate balance. Too little context, and the AI may falter, providing responses that are too general or off-target. Too much, and the AI might lose sight of the core request, buried under a mountain of details. Effective context usage requires a nuanced understanding of what information is necessary and beneficial for the AI to fulfil the request accurately.

Leveraging Context for Personalized AI Interactions

In a world where personalization is king, context is the crown jewel in AI interactions. It enables the customization of responses to fit the user's specific circumstances or preferences, leading to a more engaging and satisfying user experience. For example, the context turns a generic command like, "Play music", into, "Play music that I would like based on my recent listening history", which tailors the AI's music selection to the individual's taste.

Dynamic Context in AI Communication

Dynamic context refers to the AI's ability to understand and adapt to changing situations. It's the difference between a static one-size-fits-all response, and an intelligent situation-aware interaction. An AI that recognizes the user's current location, the time of day, or even the sentiment behind a text can provide responses that feel more intuitive and human-like.

Context as the Compass in AI Navigation

Understanding and effectively integrating context into AI prompts is crucial for creating meaningful and productive dialogues with AI. It's what turns a simple exchange of words into a rich, dynamic conversation. As we delve deeper into the anatomy of a prompt, the significance of context remains a constant, underscoring its role as the compass that guides AI in navigating the complex terrain of human communication.

Clarity

Taha Baba

The Keystone of AI Communication

Clarity in prompt design is not just a beneficial feature; it is the very keystone that supports the arch of effective AI communication. When we speak of clarity, we are referring to the unambiguous conveyance of a user's intent to the AI. It is the precision tool that carves out confusion and hones the focus on the desired outcome of an interaction.

The pursuit of precision in prompts requires a meticulous choice of language—a clear, direct expression that leaves little to interpretation. It is the difference between a vague, "Get me information", and a precise, "Find the latest research on renewable energy solutions in Europe". This distinction is critical; without clarity, an AI's response can range from marginally useful to entirely off the mark.

Crafting Crisp Communication

Crafting prompts for crisp communication with AI means favouring simplicity over complexity; specificity over generality. It's about stripping away the unnecessary so that the necessary may speak. When a prompt is clear, the AI can navigate straight to the heart of the request, bypassing the potential pitfalls of ambiguity that often trip up less carefully constructed queries.

Clarity as a Catalyst for Accurate AI Responses

In the realm of AI, clarity acts as a catalyst for accurate responses. It is the guiding force that aligns the AI's processing capabilities with the user's needs. For instance, in customer service scenarios, a clear prompt like, "Explain the return policy for electronics purchased within 30 days", immediately informs the AI of the precise information required, ensuring a relevant and succinct response.

The Art of Eliminating Ambiguity

The art of eliminating ambiguity in AI prompts is a skill that demands both understanding of the AI's capabilities and insight into the user's context. It's a balancing act of providing just enough information to guide the AI without overwhelming it with unnecessary details. It's about being concise but complete, straightforward but not oversimplified.

The Art of Clarity in AI Dialogues

In summary, clarity is the cornerstone of effective communication with AI. It is the critical element that ensures AI understands and executes on user prompts as intended. As we continue to dissect the anatomy of a prompt, the role of clarity stands out as a fundamental driver of successful AI interactions— essential for achieving precise, accurate, and valuable exchanges between humans and machines.

Taha Baba

Cohesion

Weaving the Fabric of AI Dialogue

Cohesion in prompt design refers to the element that weaves individual pieces of communication into a seamless dialogue, ensuring that each prompt naturally connects to previous interactions and guides AI responses accordingly.

Cohesion is essential for maintaining a logical flow within AI conversations. It ensures that each prompt builds upon the last, creating a coherent narrative rather than a disjointed exchange. For example, if a user is inquiring about a complex process like applying for a mortgage, a cohesive prompt might include reference to previous questions, such as, "Given the interest rates we discussed, what would be the estimated monthly payment for a 30-year fixed mortgage?".

The Role of Memory in AI Prompts

To achieve cohesion, prompts must sometimes incorporate elements of memory, referencing past interactions. This can involve callbacks to earlier parts of the conversation or even to past interactions, depending on the sophistication of the AI system. Such references can help the AI to understand the context better and provide more accurate and relevant responses.

Structuring for Clarity and Continuity

Crafting prompts that are structured for clarity and continuity is a balancing act. The goal is to provide enough information to guide the AI without overwhelming it with extraneous details. This is particularly important in service-oriented AI applications, where users might engage in prolonged conversations to resolve their issues.

Bridging the Gaps Between AI and Human Understanding

Cohesion also acts as a bridge between AI and human understanding, accounting for the differences in processing information. Humans naturally use previous conversation points to inform their current understanding, and cohesive prompts enable AI to mimic this process more effectively.

Crafting a Tapestry of Dialogue

In short, cohesion is about crafting a tapestry of dialogue where each thread is purposefully placed to enhance the overall pattern of conversation. It's a critical aspect of prompt design that ensures AI conversations are not a series of unconnected statements, but a fluid and logical interaction that feels natural to the user. Through careful design that takes into account the flow and connection between prompts, we can guide AI to interact in ways that are increasingly sophisticated and satisfying for the user.

Taha Baba

Calibration

Tuning the AI to Human Frequencies

Calibration in the context of AI prompt design is akin to tuning a musical instrument to ensure it plays in harmony with others. It involves fine-tuning the AI's responses to align closely with human expectations and the subtleties of human communication.

In addition, calibration requires a careful consideration of user feedback. By analyzing how users interact with the AI, designers can adjust prompts to better suit the users' needs. For example, if users frequently follow up for clarification on a particular prompt response, this indicates a need for recalibration to make the initial response clearer.

Contextual Sensitivity

A well-calibrated prompt is sensitive to the context. It accounts for the user's current state, previous interactions, and the overall goals of the dialogue. Contextual calibration ensures that the AI can participate in conversations as naturally as possible, providing relevant and timely information that feels intuitive to the user.

Language and Tone Adjustment

Language and tone are critical elements of calibration. The AI must match the user's language complexity, use industry-specific terminology appropriately, and adjust its tone according to the conversation's emotional undercurrents. This level of calibration can make the difference between an AI that feels robotic and one that seems almost human.

Continuous Improvement

Calibration is not a one-time process but an ongoing one. As user needs evolve and AI technology improves, the prompts must be recalibrated to maintain the quality of interactions. This continuous process of adjustment and improvement is what keeps the AI relevant and effective.

The Dynamic Dance of Calibration

Finally, calibration is a dynamic dance that requires prompt designers to be in tune with both the AI's capabilities and the users' needs. It's about continuously adjusting the AI's responses to achieve a harmonious interaction that resonates with users. By keeping the AI calibrated, we can ensure that it remains a valuable and efficient conversational partner that enhances the user experience.

Taha Baba

Examples Illustrating Components of a Prompt

Delving into the anatomy of a prompt is akin to exploring the inner workings of a clock. Each cog and wheel play a crucial role in the overall function. In the realm of AI, these components are the building blocks of effective communication. Through practical examples, we can illuminate the significance of each element within a prompt's structure. Some of these illustrations are as follows:

Customer Service Inquiry

Imagine a customer service AI designed to assist with online shopping queries.

Command: "Help me track my order".
The command is direct and action-oriented, signalling the AI to retrieve order tracking information.

Context: "I placed an order last Friday with express shipping".
By providing context, the prompt includes essential details about the order date and shipping method, allowing the AI to tailor its response accordingly.

Clarity: "What is the current status of my delivery?"
This prompt is clear and specific, eliminating ambiguity about the information sought.

Creativity: "Can you give me an update on my order in the style of a weather report?"
Injecting creativity, this unusual request challenges the AI to deliver information in a novel, engaging format.

Language Learning Application

Consider an AI language learning application prompting users to practice new vocabulary.

Command: "Construct sentences using the word 'serendipity.'"
The command here instructs the AI to prompt the user for sentence construction, a clear call to action.

Context: "The word 'serendipity' often describes happy accidents".
The context gives the user a definition to guide sentence creation.

Clarity: "Write a sentence about a serendipitous event during a vacation".
This prompt is clear, guiding the learner to use the new vocabulary in a specific scenario.

Creativity: "Imagine you found a treasure map. Describe your serendipitous discovery in a short story".
Creativity is leveraged to make the learning process more engaging and memorable.

Taha Baba

Personal Assistant AI

Envision a personal assistant AI designed to help with daily scheduling.

Command: "Schedule a meeting".
The command initiates the action of creating an appointment.

Context: "I have a dental appointment next Wednesday at 3 PM".
Providing context, the prompt specifies the exact timing and nature of the appointment.

Clarity: "Remind me about my dental appointment one day in advance".
The clarity of the prompt ensures that the AI understands when the reminder should be set.

Creativity: "Create a reminder for my appointment that sounds like an invitation to an adventure".
The creative aspect makes routine task management more enjoyable.

Synthesizing the Elements for Mastery

In crafting prompts for AI, the balance between command, context, clarity, and creativity is paramount. Like a maestro conducting an orchestra, each element must harmonize with the others to create a symphony of seamless interaction. These examples serve as a blueprint for designing prompts that effectively communicate intent, engage users, and harness the full potential of AI technologies. Through these illustrations, we gain a deeper appreciation for the nuanced craft of prompt design—a craft that, when mastered, can elevate the ordinary into an art form.

The journey through the anatomy of a prompt is much like assembling a mosaic. Each piece—command, context, clarity, and creativity—must interlock precisely to reveal the complete picture. As we conclude this chapter, we reflect on the essence of prompt design as an art form that marries technical precision with creative intuition. Command is the anchor, a clear directive that propels the AI towards a specific function. Context is the compass, offering direction and nuance to navigate the vast seas of possibilities AI can explore. Clarity is the lens through which the AI perceives our requests, focusing its capabilities to match our intentions with pinpoint accuracy. Creativity, then, is the flourish—the unique human touch that transforms a routine exchange into an engaging and memorable experience.

Throughout this chapter, we have dissected prompts to understand their fundamental components. We have learned that an effective prompt is more than a mere question or command; it is a crafted instrument tuned to elicit the most coherent and relevant responses from AI. By examining diverse examples, we have seen how varying one element can alter the outcome, much like how a single note can change a melody. As we move forward, the insights gleaned here will serve as a foundation for building more advanced, nuanced, and effective prompts. The knowledge of what makes a prompt not just functional but exceptional is what will set apart proficient AI communicators from novices. The art of prompt perfection lies in the subtle balance of its elements. Mastery of this art will empower us to unlock the full potential of AI conversations, enabling us to craft interactions that are not just efficient, but also enriched with the depth and dynamism of true human-AI synergy.

Taha Baba

Designing Effective Prompts

Mastering the Art of Clarity and Brevity in Prompt Design

In the realm of AI communication, clarity and brevity are the twin pillars upon which effective prompt design is built. The capacity to convey complex ideas succinctly is not just a linguistic skill, but a strategic one, that directly impacts the efficiency and success of AI interactions. This section of the book underscores the vital importance of mastering these aspects, providing a pathway to crafting prompts that are not only understood but also acted upon with precision by AI.

Clarity
The Beacon of Understanding

Clarity in prompts is the beacon that guides AI through the fog of potential misinterpretation. It involves distilling the essence of a request into its most comprehensible form, ensuring that AI can grasp the intent without ambiguity. This is critical because AI, by its current design, lacks the nuanced understanding of human communication. It thrives on clear, direct input to provide equally clear and direct output.

A clear prompt avoids misunderstandings, reduces the need for follow-up clarifications, and enhances the overall user experience. It ensures that AI can process requests without confusion, paving the way for a smooth and effective dialogue.

Brevity
The Soul of Wit in AI Dialogue

Brevity is equally important. Shakespeare famously said, "Brevity is the soul of wit", and in the context of AI, it is the soul of efficacy. The goal is to eliminate unnecessary verbosity without sacrificing the completeness of the message. A concise prompt helps maintain AI's focus on the task at hand and prevents it from veering off into irrelevant tangents.

Achieving brevity without losing clarity is a balancing act. It requires a deep understanding of the AI's capabilities and limitations, as well as the user's needs. It's about finding the shortest path to understanding without leaving out essential signposts along the way.

Taha Baba

The Interplay of Clarity and Brevity

The interplay between clarity and brevity can be seen in the difference between, "Tell me what you can about the historical significance of the Roman Empire", which is clear but not brief, versus, "Summarize the impact of the Roman Empire", which maintains clarity while being succinct. Effective prompts often hinge on the strategic use of: keywords that AI is trained to respond to, the careful structuring of sentences to avoid ambiguity, and the avoidance of complex phrases that could confuse the AI.

Practical Illustrations and Exercises

The subsequent sections will offer practical illustrations and exercises that encourage the reader to experiment with crafting prompts. These examples will demonstrate how subtle changes in wording can significantly alter AI's responses. The exercises will challenge readers to refine their prompts, cutting away the superfluous to reveal prompts that are both crystal clear and admirably concise.

Mastering the art of clarity and brevity in prompt design is not just about improving individual interactions with AI. It's about contributing to the evolution of AI conversational agents, making them more accessible and effective for a broader user base. As AI continues to permeate various facets of daily life, the ability to communicate effectively with AI through well-designed prompts becomes increasingly valuable. This section lays the groundwork for readers to become adept at this critical skill, ensuring that their dialogue with AI is as productive and meaningful as possible.

Principles of Clear Communication in AI

In the labyrinth of digital discourse, the principles of clear communication in AI stand as vital touchstones, ensuring that interactions are not only effective but truly transformative. This section of "The Art of Prompt Perfection: Mastering AI Conversations" is devoted to unravelling these principles, providing readers with the keys to unlock the fullest potential of AI through the power of well-crafted prompts.

The Foundation of AI Dialogue

Clear communication with AI is predicated on a foundation built on precision and adaptability. It requires a keen understanding of the AI's linguistic framework and an appreciation of the end goal of the interaction. To communicate effectively with AI, one must:

Be Explicit
AI lacks the human ability to read between the lines, so clarity comes from being explicit in your prompts.

Taha Baba

For example, instead of saying, "I need to get there fast", specify, "What is the quickest route to the airport using public transportation?".

Use Simple Language

Complex sentences and jargon can confuse AI. Simple, direct language ensures that the AI can process and respond to requests without misinterpretation.

Avoid Ambiguity

Ambiguity is the archnemesis of clear AI communication. Ensure prompts are unambiguous to prevent AI from making incorrect assumptions or requiring additional clarification.

Structuring AI Prompts for Maximum Clarity

The structure of your prompt can greatly influence how AI interprets and responds to it. For instance:

Sequential Structure

When giving instructions or seeking information that involves a sequence, structure your prompt in a step-by-step format. "First, how do I lock the device, and second, how can I secure my data remotely?"

Hierarchical Structure

When the prompt involves complex information, a hierarchical structure, starting from the general and moving to the specific, can help the AI provide organized and digestible responses.

The Role of Feedback Loops

Clear communication with AI is not a one-way street. Establishing feedback loops where the AI confirms understanding or seeks clarification is crucial. This principle helps refine the interaction process, ensuring that the AI's responses are on target.

Confirmation Requests

After receiving a response, ask the AI to confirm or summarize the information to ensure accuracy. "To confirm, you're suggesting the best time to visit is in May, correct?".

Incremental Information Disclosure

When faced with complex tasks, provide information incrementally to avoid overwhelming the AI. Start with a broad prompt and narrow down as the AI follows up with questions.

Taha Baba

Real-World Application and Best Practices

Implementing these principles in real-world scenarios significantly improves the utility and satisfaction derived from AI interactions. Whether it's customer service chatbots, virtual assistants, or complex analytical AI, the application of clear communication principles is universal.

Consistent Terminology

Use consistent terms and phrases throughout interactions to help AI maintain context and reduce errors.

Cultural Sensitivity

Be aware of cultural differences in communication that may affect the AI's interpretation of prompts and its responses.

The art of communicating clearly with AI is a skill that, once honed, opens up a world of possibilities. It is a fundamental aspect of prompt design that directly impacts the performance, usability, and reliability of AI systems. This section has laid out the core principles and strategies to guide readers in shaping their prompts to engage in more meaningful, productive, and seamless conversations with AI. With these tools, readers are empowered to navigate the nuances of AI dialogue, leading to interactions that are not only understood but are truly engaging and effective.

The Power of Precision in Prompt Design

Precision in prompt design is like the sharpening of a lens, bringing the desired response into clear focus. In the realm of AI, where every word can alter the trajectory of a conversation, the exactitude of a prompt is paramount. This section explores the compelling effect of precision on AI's ability to interpret and respond to human input with accuracy and relevance.

Crafting Precision in AI Prompts

The essence of precision lies in the meticulous choice of words and the construction of the prompt. It's a deliberate effort to eliminate vagueness and generalities, ensuring that each prompt carries a clear and direct signal to the AI about the expected outcome. For example:

Exact Language

Using specific terms rather than general ones can significantly change the AI's response. "Show me the balance of my checking account", as opposed to, "How much money do I have?", will yield a direct and clear answer.

Taha Baba

Detailed Inquiry

Incorporating relevant details can refine the AI's search parameters, resulting in more tailored information. "What's the weather forecast for downtown Seattle on July 4th?", provides the AI with three specific criteria: location, date, and type of information.

The Impact of Specificity on AI Efficiency

Specificity is the beacon that guides AI through the vast sea of data, allowing it to filter out the noise and hone in on what matters. When prompts are precise:

Response Time

AI can process and respond more quickly as the scope of the search is narrowed down, increasing efficiency and user satisfaction.

Relevance

The relevance of the AI's responses improves with the level of detail in the prompt, as it can better align its outputs with the user's intent.

Practical Examples of Precision in Action

Real-world applications of precision in prompt design showcase its undeniable value:

Customer Service

A precise prompt in customer service, such as, "I received my order of red sneakers, size 8, but I need to exchange them for a size 9", immediately directs the AI to provide exchange instructions for the specific item.

Technical Support

In technical support, a prompt like, "My Aspire 5 laptop is not connecting to Wi-Fi after the latest update", enables the AI to focus on a solution for a specific model and issue.

Precision in prompt design is not a mere luxury, but a necessity in the dance of human-AI interaction. It empowers AI to operate with a level of accuracy and relevance that resonates with the user's needs. As we delve deeper into the sophistication of AI, the power of precision will remain a critical factor in crafting prompts that are clear, concise, and result oriented. This section has illuminated the path to achieving such precision, offering readers the insight to craft prompts that elicit the best AI has to offer, thereby maximizing the potential of every interaction.

Taha Baba

Illustrative Examples of Clear vs. Complex Prompts

Navigating the intricacies of human-AI communication hinges on the ability to construct prompts that are both effective and accessible. This subtlety in prompt design can be the difference between an AI that merely functions and one that flourishes. Let's delve into the contrast between clear and complex prompts to understand why simplicity often trumps complexity.

The Clarity Spectrum in Prompt Design

Clear prompts are the keystones of successful AI interactions. They are direct, devoid of ambiguity, and serve a singular purpose. Complex prompts, by contrast, are multifaceted and can lead to confusion, often resulting in less effective outcomes. For example:

- Clear Prompt: "Set a reminder for my dentist appointment at 3 PM tomorrow".

- Complex Prompt: "I'm going to see the dentist, and I don't want to forget, so maybe put something in my calendar or something?".

The clear prompt tells the AI exactly what to do and when. The complex prompt leaves room for interpretation, which could result in the AI asking follow-up questions or not setting the reminder correctly.

Demonstrating Effectiveness Through Comparison

To illuminate the importance of clear prompts, consider the following scenarios where AI's response quality is directly tied to the clarity of the input:

- Simple Task Request: "Turn on the living room lights", vs., "It's really dark in here, can you do something about the lights?".

- Information Retrieval: "What is the capital of France?", vs., "I was wondering about big cities in France, like where the government is based?".

In the first scenario, the clear prompt will likely result in immediate action, while the complex prompt may not trigger the desired response. In the second, the clear prompt yields a straightforward answer, whereas the complex prompt could lead to a broad discussion about French cities without ever answering the initial implied question.

The Role of Precision in AI Responsiveness

Precision is not just about brevity, but about crafting prompts that guide AI to respond in a way that aligns with our intentions. Consider:

- Product Inquiry: "What are the features of the iPhone 12?", vs., "I'm thinking about phones, maybe iPhones, or something else, what do you know?".

The precise prompt leads to a specific and detailed response about the iPhone 12, while the vague prompt could result in a generic discussion about smartphones. The juxtaposition of clear versus complex prompts serves as a practical guide for effective AI interaction.

Through these illustrative examples, we have seen that the power of a well-crafted prompt lies in its clarity. By embracing simplicity and specificity, we can harness the full potential of AI, ensuring that our digital conversations are as fruitful and efficient as those we have with our fellow humans. This chapter has shed light on the pivotal role of prompt clarity in achieving meaningful and productive AI interactions, a cornerstone in the pursuit of prompt perfection.

Navigating the Spectrum of Prompt Specificity in AI Conversations

The art of prompt crafting in AI interactions lies not just in asking questions, but in the delicate balance between vagueness and specificity. Striking the perfect chord can significantly amplify the effectiveness of AI, while missing the mark can lead to frustration and miscommunication.

The Balance Beam of Specificity

In the realm of AI, the specificity of a prompt can be visualized as a balance beam, where one side represents an overly broad request and the other an excessively detailed directive. The sweet spot is in the middle, where the prompt is clear enough to be understood but flexible enough to accommodate the AI's creative or analytical strengths.

For instance, consider the differences in these prompts when searching for a dinner recipe:

- Vague: "I need a dinner recipe".

- Specific: "Provide a recipe for a gluten-free, vegan lasagna that takes less than one hour to prepare, using no more than ten ingredients".

Taha Baba

The vague prompt could yield an overwhelming array of options, while the overly specific prompt might limit the AI's ability to provide alternative recipes that might be of interest. A balanced prompt might be, "What are some quick vegan dinner ideas?"

The Role of Context in Specificity

Context is the lens through which AI interprets the specificity of a prompt. Without context, even a specific prompt can be misunderstood. With it, even broad prompts can yield surprisingly precise results. For example, "Show me financial news", can lead anywhere. But if the AI knows you're a tech investor, it might show you the latest in tech IPOs, venture capital trends, and market analysis.

The Dangers of Over-Specification

Over-specification can be as detrimental as being too vague. It can constrict AI's ability to use its full capabilities, leading to a narrow set of results that may miss valuable insights. Imagine asking an AI trained in literary analysis to, "Analyze the use of the word 'blue' in chapter three of 'The Great Gatsby'". While specific, it overlooks the AI's capacity to provide a comprehensive thematic analysis.

The key to crafting the optimal prompt lies in understanding the capabilities of the AI and the goals of the interaction. Is the intent to gather information, seek a solution, or generate creative content? Knowing this, one can adjust the specificity of the prompt accordingly.

Practical Application in Business Intelligence

In business intelligence, specificity in prompts is critical. A prompt like, "How did sales perform last quarter?", might be too broad. In contrast, "Compare last quarter's sales figures for product X in region Y to the previous year", gives the AI a clear direction, leading to actionable insights.

To conclude, navigating the spectrum of prompt specificity is an art that requires calibration. As we continue to engage with AI, it becomes apparent that the right amount of specificity can unlock the vast potential of AI, leading to more effective and meaningful interactions. The prompts we design serve not only as questions but as bridges between human intent and AI capability, and the mastery of this balance is essential for anyone looking to excel in the field of AI conversations.

Achieving the Optimal Balance in Prompt Design

Crafting the perfect prompt in AI conversations is akin to an art form—one that requires a nuanced understanding of when to detail and when to embrace openness. The right balance can elicit the best of AI's abilities, while a misstep can lead to underwhelming or misaligned responses. In this section, we delve into the principles that underpin this intricate balancing act.

The Interplay of Detail and Openness

The most effective prompts are those that manage to convey sufficient detail to guide AI while leaving enough open space for the system's algorithms to fill in gaps with innovation or breadth. It's about understanding the exact needs of the moment and the capabilities of the AI you're engaging with. An overly detailed prompt might constrain the AI, limiting its responses to a narrow corridor of possibility. Conversely, too much openness may result in a flood of irrelevant information.

Consider the needs of a user seeking investment advice:

- Overly Detailed: "What are the precise steps I should take to rebalance my stock and bond portfolio today?"

- Overly Open: "How do I invest?"

A balanced prompt would be, "What strategies can I consider for rebalancing my portfolio in a volatile market?"

Crafting with Context

Understanding the context in which AI operates is essential for balancing detail and openness. The context includes not just the immediate conversational history but also the broader environment in which the AI and user are situated. In a business setting, for example, an AI might be expected to understand industry jargon and integrate that into its response strategy. The following are examples of this balancing act:

In Customer Service: A customer service AI needs to strike a balance between understanding the problem and providing solutions without overwhelming the customer. A prompt like, "What issue can I assist you with regarding your recent transaction?", strikes this balance better than either, "What's wrong?" or "Please provide the transaction ID, the date, the amount, and the nature of your issue".

In Healthcare: AI designed for healthcare support must balance medical accuracy with patient understanding. A prompt such as, "Can you describe your symptoms and when they began?", offers a balance that allows for an accurate yet patient-friendly interaction.

Taha Baba

Balancing for Different AI Models

Different AI models, due to their unique architectures and training data, may require different approaches to balance. A model trained on encyclopaedic data might handle detailed prompts well, while a conversational model might excel with open-ended questions. Achieving balance in prompt design is not a one-time act, but a continuous process of refinement. It involves constant tuning and feedback, learning from each interaction to refine the prompts further.

Impact on User Experience

The right balance in prompt design directly impacts the user experience. It's the difference between an AI that seems almost clairvoyant in its understanding and one that seems obtuse or oblivious.

In essence, the optimal balance in prompt design is about harmonizing the AI's computational abilities with the human need for relevance and precision. It's about crafting a path that leads to the heart of the matter without foreclosing opportunities for discovery or clarity. As we continue to explore the vast potential of AI, the ability to strike this balance becomes a foundational skill for anyone looking to leverage AI effectively. It is here, in the nuanced dance of specificity and openness, that the true art of prompt perfection lies.

Contextual Considerations in Prompt Design

The role of context in shaping AI responses cannot be overstated. Context is the fabric that weaves together the disparate elements of communication, giving meaning and direction to the interaction. In the realm of AI, context serves as the cornerstone of prompt design—a critical factor that determines the relevance and applicability of the AI's response.

Understanding Context in AI

In AI prompt design, context encompasses a broad spectrum of elements, from the user's history with the AI system to the situational nuances of the conversation. It's the difference between a response that is generically accurate and one that is uniquely tailored to the user's current circumstances. For instance, a weather query without context yields a general forecast, but the same query with the addition of a location becomes a valuable piece of information tailored to the user's needs.

Context in AI is multidimensional. It includes:

Taha Baba

- Temporal Context: Refers to the timing of the interaction, which could affect the response. For example, "What are today's news highlights?" versus "What were the main events last week?".

- User Context: Involves understanding the individual user's preferences, past behaviours, and potential expectations.

- Environmental Context: Takes into account the physical or digital environment from which the prompt originates.

Embedding Context in Prompts

Embedding context in prompts is about more than just data. It's about understanding the user's world and reflecting that understanding back through the AI's responses. It is a dance of subtlety and precision, requiring a deep understanding of both the user and the AI's capabilities. AI systems can dynamically adapt to context, but they need prompts that are designed to allow for such flexibility. A prompt like, "Tell me how to prepare for my day", can lead to a wide range of responses based on the user's calendar, weather, and personal habits.

Contextual Clues and AI Response Quality

The quality of an AI's response often hinges on the contextual clues provided in the prompt. Without these clues, the AI's responses can seem out of touch or irrelevant. But with them, the AI can demonstrate a surprising level of insight and usefulness.

Cultural context also plays a vital role in prompt design. Prompts must be culturally sensitive and adaptable to different norms and values to be truly effective on a global scale.

Case Studies in Contextual Prompt Design

- E-commerce Chatbot: An e-commerce chatbot uses contextual prompts to suggest products based on a user's browsing history and past purchases, enhancing the shopping experience.

- Healthcare Assistant: A healthcare AI assistant relies on contextual prompts related to a patient's medical history to provide personalized health recommendations.

Contextual Design Strategies

Strategies for incorporating context into prompt design include:

Taha Baba

- Explicit Context: Directly embedding relevant details within the prompt.

- Implicit Context: Relying on the AI's ability to infer context from previous interactions or known user data.

AI systems learn from each interaction, and the context provided in prompts is a significant part of that learning process. Over time, an AI can become more adept at understanding and utilizing context if the prompts are designed to facilitate this learning.

The Future of Context in AI

As AI technologies evolve, the ability to understand and utilize context is only going to become more sophisticated. Future AI systems will be able to discern context from increasingly subtle cues, leading to even more nuanced and relevant interactions.

Lastly, the role of context in prompt design is a dynamic and integral aspect of AI interaction. By carefully considering the various dimensions of context, designers can create prompts that guide AI systems to respond in ways that are both meaningful and helpful to users. Context is not just a background element—it's a critical factor that can make or break the efficacy of AI communication.

Real-World Examples of Specific vs. Open Prompts

The distinction between specific and open prompts in AI communication is more than academic—it directly influences the effectiveness of AI interactions in real-world applications. To illustrate this, we'll explore scenarios where the level of specificity in prompts dramatically alters the outcome.

Specific Prompts in Customer Service

In a customer service setting, specific prompts can transform a frustrating user experience into a swift resolution. For instance, a user seeking help with a product issue might engage with an AI chatbot. An open prompt like, "What can I help you with?", may yield an array of general responses, adding to the user's frustration. In contrast, a specific prompt such as, "Tell me about the issue you're facing with your product model X500", immediately narrows down the conversation to pertinent details, allowing the AI to provide a focused solution.

Taha Baba

Open Prompts in Creative Industries

Conversely, open prompts find their strength in creative industries where flexibility and innovation are desired. For example, in a brainstorming tool used by advertisers, an open prompt like, "Generate campaign ideas for a lifestyle brand", invites a variety of creative concepts. The ambiguity allows the AI to explore a wide creative space, producing diverse and innovative ideas that might not have been considered with more restrictive, specific prompts.

Specificity in Healthcare

In the healthcare domain, specific prompts can be crucial. An AI-powered diagnostic tool prompted with, "Analyze the patient's symptoms and provide possible conditions", could return a broad range of medical conditions. However, if the prompt includes specific symptoms and patient history, such as, "Analyze the patient's chronic cough and weight loss", the AI can offer a more accurate differential diagnosis, potentially including conditions like tuberculosis or lung cancer.

Open Prompts in Educational Tools

Educational platforms leverage open prompts to encourage comprehensive learning. A prompt like, "Discuss the events leading to World War II", can prompt an AI tutor to provide a broad overview, encouraging students to explore various aspects of history. This open-ended approach fosters critical thinking and allows students to discover connections between historical events.

E-commerce Personalization

E-commerce platforms exemplify the balance of prompt types. A specific prompt might be, "Show me blue running shoes in size 10", leading the AI to display a narrow selection. An open prompt like, "Suggest gift ideas for a friend who likes sports", allows the AI to present a wide array of options, appealing to different tastes and potentially increasing sales through discovery.

AI in Content Curation

Content curation is a technique that involves finding, organizing, and sharing relevant and valuable information on a specific topic or niche. Unlike content creation, which involves producing original content from scratch, content curation relies on existing content from various sources and presents it to

Taha Baba

the audience in a meaningful way. Content curation can have many benefits for both the content creator and the audience. For example, content curation can:

- Save time and resources: Content curation can reduce the amount of time and effort required to create original content, as well as the costs associated with it. Content curators can leverage the existing content that is already available and useful and focus on adding value through their selection and presentation.
- Enhance credibility: Content curation can demonstrate the content creator's knowledge and expertise on a topic, as well as their awareness of the latest trends and developments in their field. Content curators can also acknowledge the work of other experts and give them credit, which can build trust and rapport with their audience.
- Engage audience: Content curation can offer the audience a variety of perspectives and insights on a topic, which can stimulate their interest and curiosity. Content curators can also invite the audience to share their own opinions and feedback, which can increase their engagement and retention.

In short, Content curation AI benefits from specificity when the user seeks particular information, as in, "Find articles on renewable energy trends in Europe in 2021". However, open prompts like, "Show me interesting tech news", gives a broader range of topics/trends users may not have explicitly searched for.

Navigation and Travel AI

In navigation AI, specificity ensures accuracy, as in "What's the fastest route to JFK Airport with current traffic conditions?". Open prompts, such as, "Find tourist attractions near me", enable a sense of adventure and exploration, which is essential for travel apps. In every instance, whether the prompt is specific or open, the design must be intentional, leveraging the strengths of each type to suit the interaction's goal. Specific prompts excel in situations where precision and tailored responses are required, while open prompts shine when exploration and wide-ranging possibilities are beneficial. Understanding when and how to use each type of prompt is an invaluable skill for any AI prompt designer, directly impacting the quality of AI communication and user satisfaction.

Expanding the Application of Specificity in Prompts

The application of specificity in prompts is not just about asking the right questions; it's about invoking the right kind of interaction across diverse AI scenarios. Specificity can be the bridge between a user's vague intent and an AI's precise response, facilitating a conversation that is both meaningful and actionable. Here, we focus on the ways specificity enriches AI interactions across various domains.

Taha Baba

Customer Service

In customer service, specificity in prompts can lead to increased customer satisfaction. For example, a customer looking for a refund on a late delivery would be better served with a prompt like, "I see your package was delayed. Would you prefer a refund or an expedited shipment?", rather than a generic, "How can I assist you today?". This targeted approach not only saves time but also demonstrates a business's commitment to customer care.

Healthcare

Specificity is paramount in healthcare AI applications. A prompt like, "Assess this patient's symptoms of chest pain, shortness of breath, and fatigue", enables AI to prioritize critical data, potentially identifying life-threatening conditions like myocardial infarction over less urgent concerns.

Healthcare AI extends its impact beyond diagnosis, aiding in treatment planning, medication management, and streamlining administrative tasks, such as appointment scheduling. AI-driven systems provide valuable insights to healthcare professionals, enhancing patient care and operational efficiency. In the ever-evolving field of healthcare, specificity in prompts ensures that AI serves as a powerful ally in delivering timely and accurate medical interventions.

Education

Specificity is a cornerstone of educational AI, enabling tailored learning experiences for students. Take, for example, an AI tutor prompted with, "Explain the concept of photosynthesis to a fifth grader". In response, the AI adjusts its language and examples to ensure that the explanation is accessible and age-appropriate, optimizing the learning process.

Educational AI extends its influence beyond individualized learning. It aids educators in curriculum development, adapts to students' learning paces, and provides valuable insights into student performance. Furthermore, AI-driven tools enhance accessibility for diverse learners, making education more inclusive. In the dynamic landscape of education, specificity in prompts ensures that AI becomes a valuable ally in delivering effective and personalized learning experiences for students of all ages.

Content Creation

AI is not only a powerful tool for writing blog posts, but also for generating content for various other purposes and platforms. For instance, AI can help create catchy headlines, captions, hashtags, and summaries for social media posts. AI can also produce engaging and informative content for websites, such as landing pages, product descriptions, testimonials, and FAQs. AI can even craft creative content such as poems, stories, songs, and slogans. With AI, content creation becomes faster, easier, and more diverse.

Financial Services

Specificity plays a vital role in enhancing security and accuracy in financial AI applications. Take, for instance, a prompt like, "Verify the account holder's recent transactions for any over $500 in the past 30 days". This specific prompt directs the AI's attention to significant financial activity, making it highly effective in detecting potential fraud.

Another valuable application of specificity is evident in prompts like, "Identify irregularities such as multiple transfers exceeding $1,000 within a 24-hour period in the account's transaction history". This level of detail allows the AI to swiftly pinpoint potential fraudulent behaviour, offering indispensable support to financial institutions in safeguarding their clients' assets. Including such specific prompts demonstrates the practical advantages of specificity in financial AI applications, bolstering security and trust.

Retail

Retail AI thrives on precision, and specific prompts play a pivotal role in enhancing its capabilities. Consider an AI equipped with the prompt, "Recommend products similar to a customer's recent purchases of eco-friendly goods". This level of specificity empowers AI to provide personalized shopping experiences, resulting in increased customer engagement and satisfaction.

In addition, Retail AI extends its influence beyond personalization. It contributes to inventory management, demand forecasting, and supply chain optimization. By analyzing vast amounts of data, it aids retailers in making informed decisions, ensuring that products are available when and where customers need them. Prompts like, "Who's the best supplier to get product X?", or "What is the best time to increase the stock with product X?", would increase the ROI enormously. Additionally, AI-powered chatbots and virtual assistants enhance customer support, addressing queries and concerns promptly. These multifaceted applications make Retail AI a driving force in delivering seamless shopping experiences and improving operational efficiency.

Technical Support

Specific prompts are a game-changer in technical support, significantly cutting down resolution time. Take, for instance, the prompt, "Guide the user through resetting their password on an Android device,

39

model XYZ." This level of precision ensures users receive tailored, device-specific instructions, expediting the troubleshooting process.

Beyond precision, Technical Support AI contributes to a range of support functions. It assists in diagnosing issues, providing step-by-step solutions, and even offers proactive maintenance suggestions. Additionally, AI-driven chatbots and virtual assistants are available 24/7, delivering immediate support and reducing wait times. These applications transform technical support by improving user experiences and streamlining technical issue resolution.

Marketing

Marketing AI has the remarkable capability to transform campaigns through the use of specific prompts. For instance, consider the prompt, "Analyze consumer sentiment about brand X in social media posts from the last month". This level of precision equips marketers with actionable insights that can significantly impact their strategic decisions.

By harnessing the power of AI-driven analysis, marketers gain a comprehensive understanding of how consumers perceive their brand in real-time. They can uncover trends, spot emerging issues, and identify opportunities for improvement. Additionally, AI's ability to process vast amounts of social media data within minutes provides marketers with a competitive edge in responding swiftly to market dynamics. With the aid of specific prompts, Marketing AI becomes an invaluable tool for shaping effective marketing strategies that resonate with target audiences and drive success.

Smart Home Devices

Specificity is crucial for the effectiveness of smart home AI interfaces. For example, a command such as, "Adjust the thermostat to 70 degrees at 6 PM on weekdays", prevents ambiguity and ensures a comfortable home environment when the resident arrives.

In addition to temperature control, smart home AI automates various tasks, including lighting, security, and entertainment, enhancing daily routines. These systems also promote energy efficiency, reducing utility costs and environmental impact. In the realm of smart homes, specificity in prompts ensures seamless integration, providing residents with comfort, convenience, and sustainability.

Entertainment

AI's role in the entertainment sector extends beyond content curation. While it excels in recommending tailored content with prompts like, "Find action movies rated above 7 on IMDb for a user who loves sci-fi", it also enhances the entertainment experience in various other ways.

Taha Baba

One such avenue is AI-driven personalization, where platforms analyze user preferences to recommend content that aligns with individual tastes. This goes beyond genre-based suggestions, creating a more immersive entertainment journey. Additionally, AI is instrumental in content creation, generating scripts, characters, and visual effects, transforming the filmmaking process. In gaming, AI adapts gameplay to a player's skill level, powers realistic virtual worlds, and contributes to more immersive gaming experiences.

Across these scenarios, the consistent application of specificity in prompts leads to AI interactions that are more efficient, personalized, and relevant. Whether it's providing detailed instructions, crafting individualized content, or analyzing complex data sets, the specificity in prompts is paramount in unlocking the true capabilities of AI. As AI systems continue to evolve, the art of crafting specific prompts will remain an essential skill, enabling us to communicate with machines in ways that bring forth their best performance and truly meet human needs.

Harnessing AI's Potential While Acknowledging Its Boundaries

Harnessing the potential of AI through prompt design is akin to navigating a vessel through uncharted waters: one must be keenly aware of both the strengths of the ship and the perils of the sea. In the realm of AI, this means recognizing and leveraging what AI can do well, while also being mindful of its limitations.

AI Strengths and Effective Prompt Design

AI systems, with their ability to process vast amounts of data and detect patterns, are powerful tools for a variety of tasks. Well-designed prompts can harness these strengths, directing AI to areas where it can perform with exceptional efficiency and accuracy.

For instance, when dealing with data analysis, a prompt such as, "Identify trends in customer purchase behaviour over the last quarter", plays to AI's strong suit of pattern recognition and quantitative analysis. Similarly, in language translation, a prompt like, "Translate this user manual into Spanish, maintaining technical accuracy", taps into AI's growing linguistic capabilities.

Recognizing AI's Limitations

Taha Baba

Conversely, AI's limitations often lie in tasks requiring deep understanding of context, subjective judgment, or emotional intelligence. Prompts that fail to acknowledge these limitations can lead to responses that are inaccurate or lack nuance.

For example, asking AI, "What's the best course of action for this complex ethical dilemma?", may not yield a satisfactory answer due to the subjective nature of ethics. Instead, a prompt like, "Outline potential approaches to this ethical dilemma, based on existing legal frameworks", constrains the task to AI's ability to process known data and rules, leading to a more reliable outcome.

Real-World Applications

In customer service, leveraging AI involves crafting prompts that direct the AI to provide quick, informative responses while avoiding areas of ambiguity that may mislead the user. It's crucial to emphasize that AI is a tool rather than a human replacement, designed to enhance customer support processes and streamline interactions.

For instance, consider a customer service chatbot designed to assist with troubleshooting technical issues. The prompt, "Help the customer resolve connectivity problems with their internet router", guides the AI to offer step-by-step solutions. Yet, when the customer's issue involves complex emotional nuances or unique circumstances, human intervention becomes invaluable. AI can excel in handling routine queries and tasks, but it's human agents who excel in handling intricate situations that require empathy, creativity, and a deep understanding of individual needs.

AI in Complex Environments

In complex environments, such as medical diagnosis or financial forecasting, it is crucial to design prompts that guide AI to provide data-driven insights while making clear that human expertise is needed for final decision-making. For example, a prompt like, "Compare patient symptoms with known conditions to suggest possible diagnoses", can be a valuable tool for a medical professional, provided it is used as a starting point rather than a definitive answer.

As AI continues to evolve, so too must our approach to prompt design. The future of AI prompts lies in an adaptive style that can evolve with AI's capabilities. This includes developing prompts that can grow more complex as AI becomes more sophisticated, as well as simplifying prompts when interacting with systems that have a narrower scope of expertise.

The balance between leveraging AI's potential and respecting its boundaries is delicate, but essential. It requires a deep understanding of AI's capabilities, a clear vision of the intended outcome, and a commitment to ethical and responsible AI use. By mastering the art of AI prompt design, we can unlock the full potential of AI to serve our needs, augment our abilities, and enhance our lives, all while navigating within the realm of what AI can reliably achieve.

Taha Baba

Strategies for Navigating AI Limitations

Navigating AI's limitations is a dance of strategy and ingenuity, where the choreography is designed to sidestep pitfalls and harness strengths. This subchapter endeavours to offer a repertoire of techniques to gracefully manoeuvre around AI's current limitations, ensuring that we capitalize on the technology without overstepping its current capabilities.

Identifying AI Constraints

The initial step in navigating AI limitations is to identify them accurately. This requires a comprehensive understanding of the specific AI model in use, including its training data, decision-making algorithms, and areas of proficiency. For example, recognizing that an AI's language processing may struggle with nuanced humour or sarcasm sets the stage for more effective prompt crafting.

Designing Prompts that Sidestep Limitations

Once AI limitations are identified, prompts can be carefully designed to avoid these areas. This might involve:

- Rephrasing Questions: Reformulating prompts to avoid ambiguity and to lead AI away from areas where it may falter.

- Contextual Framing: Providing a framework of context that can help AI make better sense of the query.

- Incremental Information: Breaking down complex tasks into simpler, more manageable prompts that AI can handle sequentially.

Combining AI with Human Expertise

A symbiotic relationship between AI and human expertise can address AI's shortcomings. Human oversight can ensure that AI-generated responses are vetted for accuracy and sensitivity. For instance, in content moderation, AI can flag potential issues, but human judgment is crucial to make the final call on what is appropriate.

Taha Baba

Utilizing AI as a Tool, not a Replacement

It's essential to view AI as a tool that enhances human capabilities rather than a standalone solution. For complex decision-making, AI can process and present data, but the human role in interpreting and acting on that data is irreplaceable. For example, in medical diagnostics, AI might analyze imaging to highlight areas of concern, but a trained radiologist must make the diagnosis.

Leveraging AI's Computational Strengths

AI's capabilities and limitations vary across different domains. While it may have shortcomings in certain areas, its computational prowess shines in others. Harnessing this computational strength, AI becomes a powerful ally in tasks like data mining, statistical analysis, and pattern recognition. By crafting prompts that guide AI towards these tasks, we unlock its full potential while sidestepping its weaknesses.

Consider a scenario where a financial institution needs to analyze vast datasets to detect fraudulent transactions. The prompt, "Identify unusual transaction patterns in our financial data", leverages AI's computational ability to sift through massive datasets, spot anomalies, and flag potential fraud cases. This task would be immensely time-consuming for humans but can be executed swiftly and accurately by AI.

Regular Updates and Training

As AI continues to learn and evolve, regularly updating and training AI systems can help mitigate some limitations. This might involve:

- Feedback Loops: Implementing mechanisms where AI can learn from its mistakes and successes.

- Training on Diverse Data Sets: Ensuring AI has exposure to a wide range of scenarios to improve its understanding and response accuracy.

Ethical Considerations

Navigating AI's limitations also involves ethical considerations. Ensuring that AI does not inadvertently cause harm due to its limitations is paramount. This involves:

- Transparency: Making users aware of AI's limitations.

- Safeguards: Implementing safeguards that prevent AI from making unvetted high-stakes decisions.

Taha Baba

Preparing for the Future

Finally, as we devise strategies to work around AI's limitations today, we must also prepare for the advancements of tomorrow. Staying informed about emerging AI technologies allows us to anticipate new capabilities and limitations, ensuring our strategies remain relevant and effective.

By employing these strategies, we can steer AI away from the rocky shores of its limitations and towards the open waters of its strengths, ensuring that our journey with AI remains productive, insightful, and ethically sound.

Enlightening Examples Showcasing AI Capabilities and Limitations

In the journey through the realms of artificial intelligence, it becomes pivotal to illustrate the dichotomy of AI's capabilities and limitations with real-world instances. These examples serve as beacons, guiding us to appreciate the potential of AI while remaining cognizant of its current bounds.

AI in Healthcare: Precision and Limitation

Healthcare has been a sector where AI's impact is both profound and nuanced. Take, for instance, the AI system designed to assist in diagnosing diseases from medical imaging. With the power to analyze thousands of images rapidly, the AI excels in identifying patterns imperceptible to the human eye. However, its limitation surfaces when contextual patient history or subtle symptoms that require a doctor's clinical judgment come into play. While AI can suggest potential diagnoses, it cannot replace the nuanced decision-making of a seasoned physician.

Customer Service Bots: Efficiency Meets Complexity

Customer service bots have redefined efficiency, managing inquiries at a pace no human team could match. They can resolve standard queries with unprecedented speed, but their limitations become apparent when confronted with complex customer emotions or unique problems. Here, the bot's inability to empathize or think abstractly means that a human agent's intervention is necessary to achieve a satisfactory resolution.

AI in Creative Industries: Potential Unleashed

Taha Baba

The creative industries have been a surprising beneficiary of AI, with algorithms composing music, writing poetry, and even creating art. These AI systems can generate novel creations, drawing from vast databases of existing works. Yet, they are limited by the absence of original intent or emotional depth that human artists infuse into their creations. AI may produce a technically perfect piece of music, but the soul-stirring essence that defines great art often remains elusive.

Autonomous Vehicles: Mastery and Misjudgement

Autonomous vehicles showcase AI's capabilities in navigation and real-time decision-making, safely transporting passengers by synthesizing data from various sensors. However, these systems have limitations in unpredictable environments or scenarios that require moral and ethical judgments. For instance, they struggle with the so-called "trolley problem", where a human driver's intuitive decision-making is crucial.

AI in Finance: Analysis and Anomalies

In finance, AI algorithms excel in swiftly analyzing market data, enabling predictions and rapid trades. However, they can falter in the face of anomalies or unforeseen events due to limited contextual understanding. For example, during a market crash, AI may continue using outdated models, leading to significant losses. To ensure AI's success, human oversight is vital. Experts provide context, interpret market dynamics, and make informed decisions when AI encounters unfamiliar situations. This collaboration of blending AI's speed with human insight creates a resilient financial ecosystem.

Understanding Through Contrast

By contrasting what AI can do with what it cannot, we gain a deeper understanding of its nature. It's about recognizing that AI's ability to process and analyze data is unparalleled, but its capacity for judgment, empathy, and ethical reasoning is not yet a match for human intelligence. These enlightening examples underscore the necessity of a balanced approach to AI application, leveraging its strengths while mitigating its weaknesses through human collaboration.

Preparing for Tomorrow's AI

As we consider these examples, we also look forward to developments on the horizon. Advances in AI interpretability, emotional intelligence, and ethical decision-making are areas that could see significant progress, potentially shifting the current limitations of AI and opening new avenues for its application.

In presenting these real-world instances, we aim not to constrain AI within the limits of today, but rather to prepare for its evolution. This understanding is crucial for harnessing AI's potential responsibly and effectively, ensuring that we continue to push the boundaries of what AI can achieve, all the while grounded in the reality of its limitations.

Taha Baba

Practical Applications and Real-life Examples Top of Form

Leveraging AI for Enhanced Business Solutions

The business landscape is ever evolving, and AI has become a linchpin in this transformation. Companies across the globe are leveraging AI to streamline operations, enhance decision-making, and personalize customer experiences. In this chapter, we delve into the myriad ways AI is being used to drive business innovation and efficiency.

AI in Customer Relationship Management

In the realm of customer relationship management (CRM), AI is a game-changer. With the integration of AI, businesses can predict customer behaviour, automate responses, and personalize communications at scale. For example, an AI system can analyze customer data to identify purchasing patterns, allowing businesses to tailor marketing campaigns that resonate with individual preferences. This not only increases the effectiveness of marketing efforts but also enhances the customer experience by providing relevant and timely solutions.

AI-Driven Market Analysis

Market analysis is another area where AI excels. AI algorithms can sift through vast amounts of market data to unearth trends and provide forecasts that would be impossible for a human analyst to generate in a reasonable timeframe. These insights enable businesses to make data-driven decisions, anticipate market shifts, and stay ahead of the competition. A notable instance is the use of AI in stock trading, where algorithms can execute trades based on predictive models, often with greater accuracy than human traders.

Operational Efficiency Through AI Automation

Operational efficiency is paramount in any business, and AI is at the forefront of automating routine tasks. From inventory management to scheduling, AI systems are capable of optimizing logistics to save time and reduce human error. For instance, an AI-powered logistics system can predict inventory needs, streamline supply chain processes, and even direct autonomous vehicles for delivery, thereby reducing operational costs and improving customer satisfaction.

Taha Baba

Enhanced Decision Making with Predictive Analytics

Predictive analytics is another powerful application of AI in business. By analyzing historical data, AI can predict future trends, helping businesses anticipate customer needs and market demands. This foresight is invaluable in decision-making processes, allowing businesses to plan strategically and allocate resources more effectively.

Case Studies: AI in Retail

Consider a retail giant that implemented an AI system to manage its supply chain. The AI was able to predict product demand with high accuracy, adjust inventory in real-time, and optimize delivery routes. This resulted in a significant reduction in waste, improved product availability, and increased customer satisfaction. Following are some case studies from the top leading retail brands:

Zara: A Model of AI-Driven Supply Chain Excellence

Zara stands out for its innovative use of AI throughout its supply chain. By integrating AI technologies like RFID tagging and real-time analytics, Zara has achieved an agile and responsive supply chain capable of adapting to market demands swiftly. This agility is reflected in Zara's remarkably fast design-to-store process, which allows the company to bring new designs to market in as little as one week, compared to the industry average of several months. The strategic application of AI enables Zara to optimize inventory levels and reduce waste, ensuring popular items are readily available, thereby enhancing customer satisfaction.

Key aspects of Zara's AI implementation include:

- Real-Time Analytics and Machine Learning: Monitoring and analyzing data across the supply chain to forecast demand accurately and adjust inventory levels dynamically.
- RFID Technology: Enhancing inventory visibility and accuracy, which supports better decision-making regarding stock replenishment and markdowns.
- Just-In-Telligent Supply Chain: A term reflecting Zara's advanced, AI-enhanced supply chain management approach that combines just-in-time principles with intelligent, data-driven insights.

Walmart: Reducing Food Waste with AI

Walmart's application of AI, particularly through its Eden system, exemplifies how AI can be leveraged to address specific challenges such as food waste in the retail sector. Eden uses machine learning to predict the shelf life of fresh produce by analyzing factors like temperature and humidity, which allows for more accurate demand forecasting. This capability has led to significant reductions in food waste and associated costs, with Walmart projecting savings of $2 billion over five years. Such improvements in forecasting accuracy not only benefit Walmart's bottom line, but also contribute to sustainability efforts by reducing unnecessary waste.

H&M: Tailoring Inventory to Consumer Demand

H&M's use of AI-driven demand forecasting marks a significant shift towards more data-driven decision-making in the fashion retail industry. By analyzing vast amounts of sales data, customer preferences, and

Taha Baba

market trends, H&M has improved its ability to predict future demand. This precision enables the retailer to adjust its inventory more effectively, reducing overstock and shortages. The partnership with Google Cloud is a strategic move to further enhance H&M's forecasting capabilities and supply chain management, leveraging Google's expertise in AI and machine learning to develop a dynamic and scalable platform for data-driven decisions.

The Broader Implications

The successful implementation of AI in retail operations by Zara, Walmart, and H&M showcases the potential for AI to transform traditional retail models. These examples highlight AI's role in:

- Improving Efficiency and Responsiveness: AI technologies enable retailers to respond more quickly to market changes and consumer trends, improving overall business agility.
- Enhancing Demand Forecasting: Advanced analytics and machine learning improve the accuracy of demand predictions, allowing for better inventory management.
- Reducing Costs and Waste: More accurate demand forecasting and inventory management lead to reductions in overproduction, stockouts, and markdowns, contributing to more sustainable operations.

AI's applications in business are not just enhancing existing processes; they are creating new opportunities for innovation and growth. As businesses continue to embrace AI, the potential for transformation is boundless. The examples provided in this section illustrate just a fraction of AI's capabilities in a business context, pointing towards a future where AI and human ingenuity work in tandem to achieve unprecedented levels of efficiency and customer engagement.

Transforming Educational Experiences with AI

The landscape of education is experiencing a seismic shift, thanks to the integration of Artificial Intelligence (AI). In classrooms, remote learning environments, and self-paced learning platforms, AI is not just an adjunct, but rather a central player in delivering personalized, efficient, and engaging educational experiences. This section examines the multifaceted role of AI in education, from personalized learning paths to administrative efficiency and beyond.

Personalization of Learning with AI

AI has the power to tailor educational content to the individual needs of students. Adaptive learning platforms use AI to analyze a student's performance, learning pace, and preferences to provide customized lesson plans, exercises, and feedback. This personalization ensures that students remain

Taha Baba

engaged and challenged at just the right level, maximizing their learning potential. For instance, an AI system can identify a student struggling with a mathematical concept and adapt the problem set to reinforce the fundamentals before progressing.

AI as a Teaching Assistant

AI-powered teaching assistants can handle a wide array of tasks, from grading assignments to providing quick responses to students' queries. These AI assistants can work around the clock, offering instant support and freeing up human educators to focus on more complex and creative educational tasks. An example includes an AI system that can parse through thousands of essays, providing not only grades but also constructive feedback on writing style, grammar, and argument structure.

Enhancing Engagement Through Gamification

Gamification, powered by AI, has turned learning into an interactive and enjoyable experience. AI algorithms can create dynamic learning environments that adapt to the user's interactions, offering rewards and challenges that align with the educational goals. For instance, language learning apps utilize AI to create immersive scenarios that emulate real-life conversations, making the process of language acquisition more intuitive and engaging.

Streamlining Administration with AI

On the administrative side, AI systems are streamlining processes within educational institutions. From scheduling to admissions, AI can automate and optimize operations, reducing paperwork and administrative burdens. A notable application is AI-driven analytics tools that assist in predicting enrolment trends, allowing institutions to allocate resources and staff more effectively.

Case Study: AI in Distance Learning

In the context of the global health crisis, the use of AI in distance learning has been exemplified by various platforms and initiatives aimed at facilitating remote education. While specific AI platforms were deployed across different educational institutions and countries, one notable example of technology aiding in the continuity of education during this period was highlighted by UNESCO's initiative.

UNESCO, in partnership with the International Telecommunication Union and collaboration with multiple global tech companies such as Ericsson, GIZ, Huawei, Microsoft, Norad, and ProFuturo, focused on showcasing innovative distance learning solutions during its flagship digital technologies in education event. This event, titled "Beyond Disruption: Technology Enabled Learning Futures", was organized to

Taha Baba

explore technology-enabled futures of learning, highlighting the role of AI and technology in ensuring educational continuity amid the largest education disruption in history due to the COVID-19 pandemic. The initiative aimed to share best practices and explore innovative solutions to resolve the crisis, emphasizing the creation of more resilient, flexible, and open education systems through technology and connectivity.

Another platform that made a significant impact during the pandemic is Khan Academy, which was featured during the UNESCO event for its contribution to online education through its comprehensive suite of educational tools and resources. Khan Academy's efforts were geared towards addressing the digital divide exacerbated by the pandemic and supporting the rebuilding phase of education with its online learning materials.

These initiatives underscore the critical role AI and technology have played in scaling the reach of education to students, irrespective of geographical barriers. They have facilitated interactive content delivery, monitored student engagement, and offered real-time assistance, demonstrating the potential of AI in enhancing the effectiveness and inclusivity of distance learning.

While specific teacher/student satisfaction rates regarding these AI-enhanced learning platforms during the pandemic are not detailed in the provided sources, the widespread adoption and reliance on such platforms indicate a positive reception towards using technology to maintain educational continuity in challenging times. The continued use and development of AI in education suggest a lasting impact, with potential long-term benefits for accessibility, personalized learning, and the global scalability of quality education.

AI's impact on education is profound and far-reaching. It offers opportunities for students to learn in ways that cater to their unique strengths, for teachers to provide more impactful instruction, and for institutions to operate more efficiently. The evolution of AI in education is an ongoing journey, with the promise of even more innovative applications on the horizon. The real-world instances outlined in this section showcase the potential of AI to transform educational experiences, making learning more accessible, personalized, and effective for everyone involved.

Integrating AI into Daily Life and Leisure

Artificial Intelligence (AI) has transcended the boundaries of technology and industry, weaving itself into the fabric of daily life and leisure. This omnipresence of AI has transformed mundane activities into experiences that are more efficient, enjoyable, and personalized. This section explores the breadth of AI's impact on everyday life, from smart home automation to entertainment and beyond, detailing how AI has become an indispensable ally in enhancing our daily routines.

Smart Home Automation

Taha Baba

AI has turned our living spaces into ecosystems of convenience and intuitive interaction. Smart home devices equipped with AI understand our habits and preferences, allowing for a level of automation that personalizes our environment. For example, an AI-powered thermostat learns a family's schedule and adjusts the temperature for comfort and energy efficiency. Voice-activated assistants manage tasks ranging from playing music to providing real-time updates on traffic and weather, all through natural language prompts that make interaction second nature.

Personal Health and Fitness

In the realm of health and fitness, AI applications provide personalized advice, track progress, and even offer motivation. Wearables that monitor vital signs can give insights into one's health, nudging users towards healthier habits. AI-powered fitness apps craft custom workout routines that adapt to the user's performance and goals, making personal training accessible to everyone.

Entertainment and Media

The entertainment sector has been revolutionized by AI, offering content that aligns with individual tastes. Streaming services employ AI to analyze viewing patterns, recommending shows and movies that keep users engaged. In gaming, AI not only enhances gameplay by making non-player characters more responsive and intelligent, but also tailors difficulty to the player's skill level for an immersive experience.

Culinary Exploration

In the kitchen, AI has become a culinary companion, helping to discover recipes based on dietary preferences and available ingredients. AI applications can suggest wine pairings, optimize shopping lists, and even guide users through recipes with step-by-step instructions, making cooking an interactive and fail-proof endeavour.

Travel and Exploration

AI's influence extends to travel, where it personalizes experiences from planning to actual journeys. AI chatbots assist with booking flights and accommodations, while AI-driven recommendation systems suggest destinations and itineraries tailored to the traveller's interests. During trips, AI-powered translation apps break down language barriers, enhancing the exploration of new cultures.

Taha Baba

Case Study: AI in Personal Scheduling

A notable case study is the use of AI in personal scheduling. An AI application was designed to manage a user's calendar, intelligently scheduling appointments and reminders based on priorities and preferences. The AI learned from the user's responses and adjustments, becoming increasingly adept at managing complex schedules, demonstrating the potential of AI to act as a personal time-management consultant. Among the top contenders are Clara and Trevor AI, each offering unique capabilities tailored to different scheduling needs.

Clara is praised for its human-like interaction capabilities, leveraging natural language processing to schedule meetings, manage emails, and streamline your inbox. It excels in creating a conversational and engaging scheduling experience, making it feel like you're interacting with a real person. User reviews highlight Clara's effectiveness in managing time zone differences and keeping inboxes organized, though some users note limitations without an executive plan.

Trevor AI specializes in using time-blocking technology to help manage tasks across both work and personal life. It integrates with major calendar services like Google Calendar and offers an intuitive drag-and-drop system for scheduling. Users appreciate Trevor AI for its adaptability and learning from scheduling history.

These AI assistants represent a leap forward in personal scheduling, offering tools that learn from your preferences and streamline the scheduling process. Whether you prioritize human-like interaction or the flexibility of time-blocking for task management, there's an AI scheduling assistant designed to meet those needs.

AI's integration into daily life and leisure is a testament to its versatility and user-centric design. From orchestrating the ambiance of our homes to enriching our entertainment choices and aiding in our health and culinary endeavours, AI has become an intrinsic part of our everyday existence. It not only simplifies tasks but also enriches life with new possibilities and experiences, proving that the most profound impact of technology is not just in what it does for us but how it enhances our interaction with the world around us. As we continue to explore AI's capabilities, it becomes clear that the potential for further integration into our daily lives is limited only by our imagination.

Real-World AI Implementation

The application of Artificial Intelligence (AI) across various industries has not only demonstrated its versatility but also provided valuable insights into its transformative capabilities. This subchapter explores the real-world implementation of AI through in many aspects of daily life, offering a lens through which we can observe AI's practical impact.

Taha Baba

Healthcare: AI-Enhanced Diagnostics

In the realm of healthcare, AI has made significant strides in diagnostics. A notable example is an AI system developed for detecting diabetic retinopathy, a condition that can lead to blindness if untreated. Using deep learning algorithms, the AI analyses retinal images with a high degree of accuracy, surpassing the diagnostic ability of human experts in some cases. This AI system has been deployed in remote areas, providing critical medical evaluations that would otherwise be inaccessible.

Finance: Fraud Detection Systems

The finance sector benefits from AI in the form of advanced fraud detection systems. One case study involves a major bank that integrated AI to monitor transactions in real-time, identifying patterns indicative of fraudulent activity. The AI system's ability to learn from historical data and adapt to new fraud tactics resulted in a significant reduction of unauthorized transactions, saving millions in potential losses.

Agriculture: Precision Farming

AI's reach extends to agriculture through precision farming tools that analyze data on soil conditions, weather patterns, and plant health. An agri-tech company utilized AI to provide farmers with precise recommendations on irrigation, fertilization, and harvesting, leading to increased yields and sustainable farming practices. This AI-driven approach has helped farmers optimize resource usage and improve crop quality.

Retail: Personalized Shopping Experiences

In retail, AI has redefined personalization. A fashion retailer implemented an AI system that suggests clothing items based on a customer's previous purchases and browsing history. This AI-enhanced shopping experience not only increased customer satisfaction but also boosted sales by recommending items that customers were more likely to purchase.

Transportation: Autonomous Vehicle Navigation

Autonomous vehicles represent a significant leap forward for AI in transportation. One pioneering company in this field has developed self-driving cars that use AI to interpret sensor data, navigate traffic,

Taha Baba

and learn from each trip. These vehicles are being tested in urban environments, showcasing the potential of AI to revolutionize our commute and reduce traffic-related incidents.

These case studies exemplify the real-world implications of AI across diverse sectors. AI's ability to process vast amounts of data and learn from experiences is not just enhancing existing processes but also paving the way for novel solutions to complex problems. From improving patient outcomes in healthcare to creating more efficient and personalized retail experiences, AI's real-world applications underscore its role as a catalyst for innovation. As AI continues to evolve, these case studies will serve as benchmarks for future developments, highlighting the successes and challenges of AI integration into the fabric of society.

Advanced Prompt Techniques Top of Form

Understanding and Leveraging Model-Specific Features

As the landscape of Artificial Intelligence (AI) continues to expand, the diversity of AI models available presents both opportunities and challenges in prompt design. Each model comes with its unique set of features and capabilities, which, when understood and harnessed effectively, can lead to remarkable outcomes in various AI applications. This section delves into the intricacies of model-specific features, showcasing how they can be leveraged to optimize AI interactions.

GPT Models: Creativity and Contextual Understanding

The Generative Pre-Trained Transformer (GPT) series has revolutionized natural language processing with its deep learning-based approach. GPT models excel in generating coherent and contextually relevant text, making them ideal for tasks that require a high level of creativity and nuanced understanding. For instance, when tasked with composing poetry or generating narrative prose, prompts designed for GPT models often include stylistic cues and thematic suggestions to inspire the AI's creativity while steering it within the bounds of the desired context.

BERT Models: Deep Comprehension and Information Extraction

Bidirectional Encoder Representations from Transformers (BERT) is designed to understand the context of a word within a sentence, making it especially powerful for tasks that require a deep comprehension of language structure. BERT models are adept at tasks like question answering and information extraction, where the prompt can efficiently guide the AI to focus on specific details within a text, extracting and presenting them in a user-friendly manner.

Sequence-to-Sequence Models: Translation and Summarization

Sequence-to-sequence models are designed to convert sequences from one domain to another, making them particularly useful for translation and summarization tasks. They can maintain the essence of the original content while altering its form, such as translating languages or condensing long articles into concise summaries. Prompts for these models often include explicit instructions to maintain certain aspects like tone, style, or technical accuracy, depending on the task.

Reinforcement Learning Models: Adaptation and Optimization

Reinforcement learning models learn to make decisions by receiving feedback on their actions. They are particularly useful in scenarios that require adaptation and continuous optimization, such as gameplay or real-time bidding systems. Prompts for these models focus on defining the reward structure and the desired outcomes, encouraging the model to explore and optimize its strategy towards achieving the set objectives.

Computer Vision Models: Image Recognition and Analysis

Computer vision models are trained to interpret and understand visual data. These models can perform tasks ranging from simple image recognition to complex scene analysis. Prompts for computer vision models often involve specifying the particular features or objects to be recognized or providing context for the analysis, such as identifying emotions from facial expressions or categorizing objects within an image.

Understanding the strengths and limitations of each AI model is paramount in designing prompts that can effectively leverage their specific features. By tailoring prompts to the capabilities of GPT, BERT, sequence-to-sequence, reinforcement learning, and computer vision models, AI practitioners can achieve targeted outcomes across a wide spectrum of applications. This section provides a foundation for understanding these model-specific features and highlights the importance of strategic prompt design in maximizing the potential of AI tools.

Directing AI Responses Through Strategic Prompting

In the realm of AI interactions, the ability to guide an AI towards desired responses is both an art and a strategic process. This involves understanding the AI model's workings, the context of the conversation, and the objectives of the interaction. The prompts act as a steering wheel, directing the AI along the path of a conversation, ensuring that the AI's output aligns with the user's goals.

Crafting the Path: Precise and Goal-Oriented Prompts

The precision of prompts is paramount. A well-crafted prompt provides clear direction without ambiguity, leading to a response that meets the specific needs of the user. For instance, instead of asking, "How can I manage my emails better?", a more goal-oriented prompt would be, "What are the steps to set up an automatic email filtering system?". The latter leads the AI to provide a detailed and actionable response.

Taha Baba

Contextual Cues: The Subtle Guide

Incorporating contextual cues into prompts can drastically change the AI's response. These cues provide the AI with hints about the user's current environment, historical interactions, or specific preferences. For example, the prompt, "Suggest a workout routine", might yield a general response but adding a contextual cue such as, "for someone recovering from a knee injury", tailors the AI's response to suit the user's unique situation.

Sequential Prompting: Building Conversations

Sequential prompting involves designing a series of prompts that build upon each other, guiding the AI through a conversation. This technique is useful for complex tasks that require multiple steps or when gathering information incrementally. Each prompt in the sequence narrows down the focus, honing in on the information needed and shaping the AI's responses accordingly.

Creative Constraints: Balancing Openness with Guidance

When aiming for creative outputs, such as storytelling or idea generation, prompts must strike a balance between providing freedom and offering guidance. A prompt like, "Write a story about space exploration", is open-ended whereas, "Write a story about a rogue AI on a space station, set a hundred years in the future", adds creative constraints that direct the AI's narrative construction.

Feedback Loops: Refining AI Responses

Feedback loops are a critical component of strategic prompting. They involve presenting the AI with its responses and using further prompts to refine or expand upon them. This iterative process allows for the gradual honing of AI responses until they meet the user's exact needs.

Scenario Simulation: Preparing AI for Real-World Applications

Scenario simulation with AI has been notably beneficial in customer service and emergency preparedness and response (EP&R), showcasing AI's versatility in adapting to various real-world applications.

Taha Baba

In customer service, AI's scenario simulation capabilities have been leveraged to enhance efficiency and personalization. For example, Google Cloud's Generative FAQ for CCAI Insights and Genesys Agent Assist utilize AI to automate post-call processing, significantly reducing the time agents spend on administrative tasks. These tools help contact centres understand customer intents and improve service journeys by categorizing reasons for customer contacts, generating conversation highlights, and even providing customer satisfaction scores.

In the realm of emergency management, AI has been instrumental in augmenting the capabilities of EP&R personnel. The California Department of Forestry and Fire Protection, for instance, uses image recognition AI to detect wildfires early on, aiding in quicker response and potentially saving lives and resources. Moreover, AI has been applied to monitor patient adherence to tuberculosis treatment regimens, showcasing its potential in public health crisis management.

These examples illustrate the profound impact of AI in managing complex scenarios, from improving customer service experiences to enhancing disaster response efforts. The integration of AI into these fields not only streamlines operational efficiencies but also offers a more personalized, data-driven approach to addressing individual needs and situations. As AI continues to evolve, its application in scenario simulations across different sectors is likely to expand, further demonstrating its capacity to adapt to and address a wide range of real-world challenges.

Anticipating Misinterpretations: Proactive Prompt Design

Proactively designing prompts that anticipate potential AI misinterpretations can prevent erroneous responses. This means understanding AI pitfalls and structuring prompts to avoid leading the AI astray.

Strategic prompting is a sophisticated technique that requires a deep understanding of AI behaviour, language nuances, and the objectives of the interaction. By mastering the art of prompt design, one can effectively direct AI response, ensuring they are helpful, accurate, and contextually relevant. This section has hopefully equipped you, the reader, with the knowledge and tools to refine their prompt crafting skills, enabling you to harness the full potential of AI across diverse applications.

Unleashing AI's Potential for Creativity and Innovation

The intersection of artificial intelligence with creativity and innovation is a space of limitless possibilities. AI's potential to be a partner in creative endeavours is rapidly becoming a reality. Through strategic prompt design, AI can be guided to generate novel ideas, compose music, write poetry, and even create art, thus becoming a tool for innovation across various fields.

AI models, particularly those designed for language processing and image generation, can produce outputs that are not only original but also inspire human creativity. For example, prompts that ask AI to

Taha Baba

generate ideas for a science fiction plot or to sketch the design of a futuristic vehicle can result in unique concepts that blend human ingenuity with AI's computational power.

Expanding the Horizon of AI-Driven Design

In design, AI can be used to push the boundaries of what is possible. Using prompts that encourage AI to experiment with unconventional shapes, materials, and textures can lead to the creation of design elements that are both innovative and functional. AI can also be directed to iterate on design ideas, refining them based on specific parameters or feedback.

AI in the World of Digital Art

The digital art world has embraced AI as a medium. Artists are using AI to explore new aesthetics and narratives. By feeding AI prompts that are interpretative and abstract, artists can collaborate with the AI to produce artworks that might not have been conceivable through traditional methods alone.

An intriguing example of AI in digital art is the creation of "Edmond de Belamy" by the Paris-based collective Obvious in 2018, using a generative adversarial network (GAN). This artwork, which sold for $432,500 at Christie's Auction House in New York, showcases the potential of AI to create complex and valuable art pieces. GANs, developed by Ian Goodfellow and colleagues in 2014, learn to mimic the statistical distribution of input data, such as images, allowing for the generation of new, unique artworks.

AI as a Catalyst for Musical Exploration

In music, AI can be encouraged to experiment with different genres, instruments, and harmonies to create compositions that resonate with human emotions. Prompting AI with a specific mood or theme can result in music that is both expressive and innovative, expanding the repertoire of human composers and musicians.

AIVA (Artificial Intelligence Virtual Artist) is an example of AI's impact on musical exploration, an AI designed to compose symphonic music. AIVA learns from thousands of scores of the greatest composers to generate music for movies, games, and other entertainment mediums. By analyzing patterns in music, AIVA can create compositions that evoke specific moods or themes, demonstrating AI's capability to not only mimic human creativity but also to push the boundaries of musical innovation. This example highlights how AI can serve as a tool for expanding the creative possibilities in music composition.

AI-Enhanced Storytelling

Taha Baba

The art of storytelling can be enhanced by AI when it is prompted to construct narratives with complex characters and plots. AI can be asked to write stories that address specific themes or to create characters with certain traits, resulting in narratives that are rich and engaging.

One notable example of AI-enhanced storytelling is "The Road", a narrative developed by Ross Goodwin. Using an AI algorithm, Goodwin embarked on a road trip with the AI composing the story in real-time by processing data inputs from the journey's surroundings, including images, GPS data, and even the car's movements. This experiment demonstrated the potential of AI to create unique and contextually rich narratives based on specific themes and data inputs, offering a new dimension to storytelling that intertwines technology with traditional narrative structures.

Creative Problem-Solving with AI

Beyond the arts, AI's creativity can be leveraged for problem-solving in fields like engineering and science. By prompting AI with challenges that require innovative solutions, it can assist in developing new technologies, processes, or approaches to complex problems.

AlphaFold by DeepMind would be one of the best examples of AI in creative problem-solving. AlphaFold uses AI to predict the 3D structures of proteins with remarkable accuracy. This breakthrough helps scientists understand biological processes and accelerate drug discovery by providing insights into the molecular structure of diseases. By solving this complex problem, AlphaFold illustrates AI's potential to contribute significantly to scientific and medical advancements.

Facilitating Innovation Through AI Collaboration

Collaborative environments where humans and AI work together can facilitate innovation. AI can be prompted to provide feedback on human-generated ideas or to suggest alternatives, fostering a collaborative cycle of refinement and improvement.

The potential of AI for creativity and innovation is only beginning to be tapped. As AI becomes more adept at understanding and generating human-like content, the prompts we use to guide it will become ever more crucial. By carefully crafting prompts that challenge and guide AI, we can unlock its full potential to assist and augment human creativity and innovation across countless domains. This section of the book aims to inspire readers to explore the creative capabilities of AI, and to experiment with prompt design as a means to this end.

Impact of Cultural and Linguistic Diversity on Prompt Design

Adapting Prompts for Global AI Interactions

In the global village of our digital age, AI's conversational agents transcend borders, connecting cultures and languages in a tapestry of diverse interactions. The effectiveness of AI in this global context hinges on the adaptability of prompts that consider the nuanced complexities of cultural and linguistic diversity.

Cultural competence in AI design is no longer optional; it's imperative. A conversational agent designed for international use must be sensitive to cultural norms and social etiquette. Prompts must be crafted to account for variances in politeness levels, indirectness or directness in communication, and cultural taboos. For instance, a prompt for a service bot might adjust its formality depending on whether it's interacting with users from high-context cultures like Japan or low-context cultures like the United States.

Linguistic Versatility in AI Prompts

The linguistic aspect of AI prompts must embrace diversity to cater to a global audience. This means not only translating prompts into multiple languages, but also localizing them to fit the idiomatic and colloquial nuances of each language. A prompt as simple as, "How can I help you?", when localized, could become, "¿En qué puedo asistirle?", in Spanish, employing a more formal address as is common in many Spanish-speaking cultures.

AI can serve as a bridge over the chasm of language barriers. By incorporating prompts that trigger translation services or multilingual support, conversational agents can provide real-time assistance to users in their native tongues, thereby enhancing comprehension and user experience.

AI in Multicultural Settings

Real-world case studies underscore the importance of culturally and linguistically adapted prompts. For instance, an AI travel assistant that can switch between offering succinct directions in English to providing elaborate explanations in Arabic, considering the high-context nature of Arab cultures, illustrates the versatility required for global AI interactions.

The world's cultural and linguistic mosaic demands a new breed of AI prompts—ones that are as diverse and dynamic as the human interactions they seek to emulate. By tailoring prompts to account for these differences, AI can achieve truly global reach, fostering better understanding and stronger connections across the spectrum of human diversity. This chapter will explore the strategies and considerations

Taha Baba

necessary to develop such prompts, providing readers with the insights to create AI interactions that are inclusive, respectful, and effective on a global scale.

Inclusivity and Accuracy in Multicultural AI Communication

As AI systems increasingly become a part of our global communication fabric, the design of AI prompts must advance to meet the diverse needs of a multicultural user base. Ensuring inclusivity and accuracy in AI communication is not just about avoiding misunderstandings or errors; it's about respecting cultural identities and embracing the wealth of human diversity.

Inclusivity in AI prompt design starts with recognizing the myriad ways people express themselves. It involves creating prompts that are adaptable and sensitive to cultural nuances, like variations in greeting customs or differing norms around formality and politeness. AI prompts that can adjust their language, tone, and content based on the user's cultural background can create a more welcoming and inclusive environment. For instance, a conversational agent might greet someone with, "How may I assist you today?", while opting for a more informal, "What can I do for you?", depending on cultural expectations.

Enhancing Communication Accuracy

Accuracy in multicultural communication extends beyond the correct translation of words. It encompasses the conveyance of intent, the recognition of cultural expressions, and the appropriate response to various social cues. AI systems must be equipped with prompts that encourage clarity and context-specific responses. For example, when an AI system encounters a phrase that has multiple meanings across cultures, it should use prompts to gather more context, such as "Could you tell me more about what you're looking for?"

Case studies from around the globe reveal the impact of inclusively designed AI on user satisfaction. For instance, a customer service AI that uses region-specific idioms and expressions can resonate more deeply with users, as seen in a bank's AI chatbot that employs colloquialisms unique to different Spanish dialects to assist customers from various Spanish-speaking countries.

Practical Guidelines for Multicultural AI Prompts

Creating AI prompts for multicultural communication requires a set of practical guidelines:

- Conduct thorough cultural research to inform the design of prompts.
- Involve native speakers and cultural consultants in the development process.

Taha Baba

- Test prompts with a diverse user group to identify potential issues.

- Update and refine AI models regularly to stay current with linguistic and cultural shifts.

In a world that celebrates diversity, AI prompts must be designed with an eye toward inclusivity and accuracy in every cultural context. By doing so, AI can become a tool that not only understands but also respects the rich tapestry of human communication, bridging gaps and fostering connections across cultural divides. Through this chapter, we have now explored strategies for creating prompts that honour the complexity of multicultural communication, enabling AI systems to interact authentically with users from all walks of life.

Taha Baba

Future Trends in AI and Prompt Design

Emerging Technologies in AI and Their Impact on Prompt Design

As we stand on the cusp of a new era in artificial intelligence, emerging technologies are poised to revolutionize prompt design, shaping the way we interact with AI. The relentless pace of innovation suggests that the AI of tomorrow will be remarkably different from today's models. This expansion is not merely in capacity but in capability, sensitivity, and creativity.

The advent of technologies like quantum computing and neuromorphic chips offers a glimpse into a future where AI could process information at unprecedented speeds and with a level of complexity that mimics the human brain. For prompt designers, this means crafting inputs that can leverage these advancements to produce more nuanced and sophisticated outputs. It's conceivable to have prompts that are less about directing AI and more about collaborating with it. For instance, rather than instructing an AI to perform a task, we might provide an objective or goal and allow the AI's enhanced processing capabilities to determine the best course of action.

The Interplay of AI and Emerging Technologies

Advancements in areas such as augmented reality (AR) and virtual reality (VR) are expanding the horizons of experiential learning and entertainment, where AI prompts can be designed to create immersive narratives and simulations. Imagine an educational AI prompt that doesn't just spit out facts, but rather situates the learner in an historically accurate virtual environment, complete with contextually relevant tasks and challenges.

The Role of AI in Personalizing User Experiences

With the integration of AI into the Internet of Things (IoT), we're looking at a future where AI prompts are embedded into the fabric of daily life, personalizing user experiences by understanding and predicting individual preferences and needs. The evolution of prompts will likely involve a shift from static commands to dynamic conversations that evolve based on the AI's ongoing relationship with the user.

Ethical and Practical Considerations

Taha Baba

Emerging technologies also bring forth new ethical and practical considerations for prompt design. Issues of privacy, security, and ethical decision-making will become increasingly complex, and prompt designers will need to be at the forefront of these discussions. This includes the development of prompts that are not only effective but also transparent, fair, and privacy conscious.

The future of AI and prompt design is one of boundless potential, marked by continuous evolution and transformation. As emerging technologies redefine the landscape of AI capabilities, prompt designers will play a pivotal role in shaping these interactions, ensuring that they remain not only innovative but also ethical and human-centric. The coming chapters will delve deeper into these trends, exploring the implications and opportunities they present for the field of AI prompt design and the broader sphere of human-AI collaboration.

The Role of AI Interpretability in Prompt Crafting

The quest for interpretability in artificial intelligence is a key factor influencing the future of prompt design. Interpretability, or the ability to understand and trust AI's decision-making process, is not just a technical requirement but an ethical imperative. As AI systems become more complex, the prompts that guide them must be crafted with a view to making AI's operations transparent to its users. This ensures that AI remains a trustworthy assistant, advisor, and collaborator across myriad domains.

Interpretable AI allows users to comprehend how AI systems reach conclusions or make decisions. This transparency is vital, as it underpins the users' trust, particularly in high-stakes scenarios such as healthcare diagnostics, financial forecasting, or legal assessments. Therefore, prompts must be designed to elicit explanations for AI's outputs, such as, "Explain the reasons for selecting this particular investment portfolio", or "What medical evidence supports this diagnosis?".

Prompts as Tools for Explanation

To achieve interpretability, prompts must evolve to serve as tools for explanation, not just execution. This means constructing prompts that lead AI not only to perform a task but also to articulate the rationale behind its choices. For example, in an educational context, instead of simply asking AI to, "Provide a math problem", the prompt could be, "Create a math problem and explain the concepts it is designed to test".

Balancing Complexity and Clarity

As AI systems grow more sophisticated, there is a risk that their interpretability could diminish. Prompt designers face the challenge of balancing the complexity of AI's capabilities with the clarity needed for user understanding. The prompts of the future may need to incorporate meta-information or control structures that help unpack AI's reasoning processes for the end-user.

Taha Baba

Bridging AI and Human Understanding

AI interpretability also involves bridging the gap between machine reasoning and human understanding. Prompts will need to be designed with a deep awareness of human cognitive processes, ensuring that AI's responses align with human ways of understanding. For instance, an AI prompt in a collaborative creative process might be "Describe how your suggested design elements reflect the project's intended emotional impact", encouraging AI to align its creative output with human emotional insights.

In essence, the interpretability of AI shapes how prompts are crafted, demanding a new dimension of design that accounts for the explanation, clarity, and transparency of AI processes. As AI systems advance, so too must the sophistication of our prompts, ensuring that AI remains an interpretable and trustworthy participant in our daily interactions. The subsequent sections will delve deeper into how emerging technologies will influence prompt design and the ethical considerations that accompany these advancements.

Speculative Futures: Next-Generation AI Conversational Agents

The Vision of Tomorrow's AI Conversations

As we stand on the cusp of new horizons in AI technology, the next generation of conversational agents beckons with the promise of unprecedented interactive capabilities. These agents are poised to embody advancements that push the envelope of what we consider possible today, seamlessly blending into the fabric of our daily lives.

The future of AI conversational agents lies in the synthesis of multi-modal interactions, cognitive empathy, and cultural intelligence. Emerging technologies are expected to transform AI agents into entities that can understand not just the content but the context and emotions behind human communication.

Multi-Modal Communication: A New Realm of Interaction

Next-generation AI will likely transcend the boundaries of text and voice, incorporating visual cues, gestures, and other sensory inputs to understand and convey messages. This multi-modal approach will create a more immersive and intuitive interaction, allowing conversational agents to interpret body

Taha Baba

language, facial expressions, and even the environment to tailor their responses more accurately to the user's current situation.

Cognitive Empathy: Building Deeper Connections

Cognitive empathy, the ability to understand and process the emotions of others, is a frontier that next-gen AI conversational agents are expected to explore. By integrating advanced emotional intelligence algorithms, these agents will not only recognize subtle emotional nuances in user interactions but also respond in emotionally appropriate ways, fostering a deeper connection with users.

Cultural Intelligence: Bridging Global Divides

As our world grows increasingly interconnected, conversational agents will need to display an acute awareness of cultural nuances. AI models are anticipated to evolve, incorporating diverse linguistic databases and social norms to navigate cross-cultural communications skilfully. This cultural intelligence will enable AI agents to provide more respectful and accurate interactions on a global scale.

Expanding the Role of AI in Society

The role of conversational AI is set to expand into more critical and complex sectors, from mental health support to crisis negotiation, utilizing their enhanced capabilities to provide support and solutions where human resources are limited.

Mental Health Support: A Compassionate Companion

Envision AI conversational agents capable of providing initial mental health support, identifying signs of distress, and offering coping mechanisms. They could serve as a first line of support, guiding users to professional help when necessary.

Crisis Negotiation: The AI Mediator

In high-stakes scenarios, AI agents could assist human negotiators by analyzing vast amounts of data to suggest strategies, predict outcomes, and even communicate directly in low-risk negotiations, bringing a data-driven approach to conflict resolution.

Taha Baba

Anticipating Challenges and Preparing for Change

While these advancements promise a brighter future for AI conversations, they also present challenges in ethics, privacy, and security. It will be paramount to anticipate these challenges, ensuring that next-generation conversational agents are developed with a strong ethical framework and robust security measures to protect user data and privacy.

To conclude, the future of AI conversational agents is not merely an extension of current trends but a reimagining of the interaction paradigm. As we venture into this new era, it is our collective responsibility to guide these advancements towards a future that is not only technologically advanced but also ethically grounded and culturally inclusive. The next generation of AI conversational agents stands to redefine our relationship with technology, promising an era of more meaningful and empathetic interactions.

Taha Baba

Ethical Considerations and Best Practices

Responsible AI Interaction

The interplay between AI and its human users is a tapestry woven with complex threads of ethics, each interaction a reflection of the values we hold as a society. As we craft the conversational pathways that AI will tread, ethical considerations stand as both our guide and measure. The following discourse merges the foundational elements of ethical AI interactions with the pragmatic approach to developing ethical prompts, creating a unified narrative that serves as a blueprint for integrity and responsibility in AI communication.

Foundational Ethics in AI Conversational Agents

Ethical AI begins with the intention to do good and the commitment to do no harm. This principle permeates through every layer of AI development, from the underlying code to the nuanced prompts it executes. It is a multidisciplinary commitment that integrates insights from technology, ethics, legal standards, and the diverse tapestry of human experience to ensure AI systems are just, inclusive, and aligned with the broader good of society.

Principles of Ethical AI

Creating ethical AI prompts is an art that requires a deep understanding of the principles above and a commitment to iterative design, fuelled by user feedback and continuous ethical evaluation.

To navigate the ethical landscape of AI, several principles stand as the pillars of responsible design:

1. Transparency: Users should understand how AI systems make decisions. Clarity in AI prompts facilitates trust and informed consent, ensuring users are fully aware when interacting with an AI rather than a human.

2. Fairness and Justice: AI must be impartial, offering equal access and avoiding biases. Ethical prompts are free from discriminatory language and considerate of all users, fostering inclusivity and fairness.

3. Non-Maleficence and Beneficence: AI should not mislead or cause distress. Prompts designed for AI must prioritize user safety, providing accurate information, and optimizing user well-being.

4. Privacy Preservation: AI interactions should only request necessary information, respecting the user's right to privacy and informing them of how their data will be used.

Taha Baba

5. Accountability: AI systems must have mechanisms to hold them accountable for their actions, with prompts making it clear who is responsible for AI decisions.

User-Centric and Scenario-Based Design

Prompt design must begin with the user, taking into account a multitude of potential scenarios and their ethical implications. This approach ensures that the AI assists without overstepping boundaries, such as providing medical information without infringing upon the professional expertise of healthcare providers or offering financial advice without manipulating user decisions.

Continual Feedback and Adaptation

Ethical prompts are not static; they are dynamic, evolving with user interactions and societal changes. Regular assessments and updates ensure that prompts remain ethical over time, incorporating user feedback to refine and improve the interaction experience.

The fusion of ethical AI interactions and the development of ethical prompts embodies a comprehensive mandate for the responsible use of technology. This unified approach ensures that AI systems not only serve the immediate needs of users but do so with an unwavering commitment to the ethical principles that uphold our societal values. AI systems designed with these considerations at the forefront stand to benefit humanity, enhancing user experiences and promoting a future where technology and ethics coalesce to enrich lives and advance society.

Case Studies in Ethical Prompt Implementation

Real-world implementations of ethical AI provide concrete examples of these principles in action:

Case Study 1: Healthcare AI - Ethical Interaction in Patient Support

Healthcare AI systems have the potential to revolutionize patient care by providing timely information and support. However, the sensitive nature of health-related data demands a particularly ethical approach to prompt design. In one notable implementation, an AI system designed to assist with patient inquiries was carefully crafted to navigate the fine line between support and diagnosis.

In this case study, akin to systems like Babylon Health and IBM Watson Health, an AI designed for patient support in healthcare navigates ethical considerations with precision. It responds to symptom inquiries by encouraging professional consultation, maintaining the crucial distinction between AI assistance and medical diagnosis. Privacy is paramount, with the AI collecting minimal information under strict adherence to HIPAA guidelines. Transparency in data handling is communicated to patients, ensuring trust and confidentiality in this sensitive domain.

To uphold privacy, the AI's prompts were also designed to collect only the minimal necessary information, using phrases like, "Please tell me only what you feel comfortable sharing. Would you like some general advice on dealing with discomfort?". This consideration not only respected patient confidentiality, but also aligned with regulations like HIPAA, which governs the privacy and security of medical information.

Ethical considerations extended to the AI's data handling procedures. Patients were informed of privacy policies through prompts such as, "Your privacy is important. Can I explain how we handle your health data?". These measures ensured transparency and built trust between the patient and the AI system, which is crucial in the healthcare setting where the stakes are inherently high.

Case Study 2: Financial Advisory AI - Fairness in Economic Decision-Making

In the financial sector, AI can provide valuable assistance to users looking to manage their finances or make investment decisions. However, ethical considerations are paramount to ensure fairness and avoid the exploitation of user vulnerabilities. A financial advisory AI system was developed to assist users with varying degrees of financial literacy, which posed a unique challenge in prompt design.

Real-world examples like PayPal and Wealthfront highlight the practical application of AI to ensure fairness and improve decision-making. PayPal utilizes machine learning algorithms for real-time risk assessment and fraud detection, scanning transactions and automatically flagging suspicious activities. This application of AI helps protect users from fraudulent transactions, showcasing AI's capacity to make quick, accurate assessments that benefit the user base broadly.

Wealthfront, on the other hand, leverages AI to offer personalized investment advice through its platform. By considering a customer's risk tolerance, goals, and preferences, Wealthfront's AI-driven platform can create optimized investment portfolios tailored to individual needs. This approach empowers users to make informed financial decisions without the influence of bias, ensuring that recommendations are based solely on the user's unique financial situation.

Both examples underscore the ethical use of AI in financial decision-making, emphasizing the technology's potential to deliver personalized, bias-free advice and protect users from financial risks. These cases demonstrate how AI can support a range of financial activities, from safeguarding against fraud to customizing investment strategies, aligning closely with the principles of fairness and impartial guidance outlined in the financial advisory AI system described in the case study.

Additionally, the prompts could be meticulously tailored to avoid suggesting specific financial actions, thereby preventing any form of inducement or bias. For example, instead of saying, "Based on your spending habits, you should invest in X", the AI would use a prompt like, "People with similar spending habits have considered various investment options, including X. Would you like to learn more about this?". This approach empowered users to make informed decisions without unduly influencing their choices.

Taha Baba

To address the wide spectrum of financial situations and knowledge among users, the AI's prompts were designed to be inclusive and adaptable. The AI asked questions to gauge the user's familiarity with financial concepts, adjusting the complexity of the dialogue accordingly. A prompt might say, "I can provide information at different levels of detail. Would you prefer a brief overview or a detailed explanation of investment strategies?"

The AI was also programmed to recognize when a user's query fell beyond its scope of responsibility or expertise, using prompts like, "This question may be best answered by a financial advisor. Shall I help you find one?". Through these carefully crafted interactions, the AI system upheld ethical standards by providing balanced, impartial guidance, fostering an environment of fairness and trust in financial decision-making.

Case Study 3: Educational AI - Adaptive Learning and Positive Reinforcement

AI in education represents a profound shift in individualized learning, but it also raises ethical questions regarding how students are engaged and evaluated. An AI tutor system was designed to adapt to different learning styles and paces, using ethical prompts to create a supportive and encouraging learning environment.

Incorporating a real-world example, we can look at the use of AI technologies like those developed by companies such as Dragon NaturallySpeaking and Read&Write. These AI-powered tools have been instrumental in supporting students with disabilities, showcasing the adaptive learning capabilities of AI in educational settings. Dragon NaturallySpeaking, for example, offers speech recognition software that allows students with speech impairments to participate more fully in classroom activities by converting spoken words into written text. Similarly, Read&Write uses AI algorithms to assist students with dyslexia, providing features like text-to-speech and word prediction to enhance reading and writing skills.

Some institutions are already using AI-tutor, where the AI tutor is programmed to recognize a student's progress and offer prompts that are constructive and motivating. If a student made an error, the AI would respond with, "That's not quite right, but you're close! Let's try a different approach to this problem". This language was chosen to provide guidance without discouraging the learner, fostering a growth mindset.

The AI's prompts were also designed to respect the student's autonomy and pace. The system would ask, "Would you like to continue with this topic or try something new?", giving the student control over their learning journey. Furthermore, the prompts were crafted to encourage self-reflection and critical thinking, such as, "Can you tell me more about how you reached that conclusion?". This approach not only aided in knowledge retention but also encouraged the development of higher-order thinking skills.

To ensure inclusivity, the AI's language was carefully selected to be neutral and accessible to all students, regardless of background. The AI was programmed to avoid any cultural or socioeconomic assumptions, using prompts like, "I have many different examples we can use for this math problem. Which one would you like to try?". This attention to detail ensured that the AI tutor was a resource that all students could relate to and benefit from.

Taha Baba

Conclusion: Embracing the Future of AI Conversations

Reflections on AI Prompt Design

Embarking on the journey of "The Art of Prompt Perfection: Mastering AI Conversations", we have traversed the multifaceted world of AI prompt design, where the fusion of technology and linguistic acuity forms the cornerstone of effective AI interactions. The thoughtful orchestration of prompts has revealed itself to be both an intricate craft and a dynamic catalyst, pivotal to unlocking the profound capabilities of conversational agents.

In this reflective synthesis, we revisit the key insights and strategies that have emerged as guiding principles for adept prompt crafting. We have seen the power of clear, concise communication in AI prompts, ensuring that even the most advanced AI models can decipher human intent and deliver pertinent responses. The delicate balance between specificity and creativity in prompt design has been a recurring theme, highlighting the importance of tailoring prompts to the context and capabilities of the AI at hand.

As we delved into the anatomy of a prompt, it became evident that the components of command, context, clarity, and creativity are not mere ingredients but the very lifeblood of effective AI communication. Each element serves a distinct purpose: the command as the directive force, context as the situational compass, clarity as the beacon of understanding, and creativity as the spark of ingenuity. The prompts we craft are more than queries; they are the bridges between human curiosity and AI's computational prowess.

The exploration of AI's practical applications in business, education, and daily life showcased the transformative power of AI when guided by well-designed prompts. We witnessed AI's ability to enhance business solutions, transform educational experiences, and integrate into the nuances of daily life, underscoring the versatility and adaptability of AI across diverse realms of human activity.

Advanced prompt techniques presented a forward-looking approach, embracing the unique features of various AI models. These specialized strategies brought to light the importance of model-specific prompt design, ensuring that each AI's strengths are effectively harnessed, and its limitations gracefully circumnavigated. The strategic prompting that directs AI responses and the unleashing of AI's potential for creativity and innovation stand as testaments to the boundless possibilities inherent in the realm of AI.

In a world rich with cultural and linguistic diversity, the impact of these factors on prompt design was acknowledged with the aim of fostering global AI interactions that are inclusive and accurate. The role of AI interpretability in prompt crafting was underscored, emphasizing the necessity for transparency and trust in AI's decision-making processes.

Taha Baba

As we speculate on the future of AI and prompt design, we recognize that emerging technologies will bring forth a new epoch of conversational agents. These next-generation agents will likely be marked by a deeper understanding of human emotions, cultural contexts, and the ability to engage in multi-modal communication. The ethical considerations and best practices discussed serve as a compass for navigating this future, advocating for responsible AI interactions and the development of ethical prompts.

Anticipating the Future of AI and Conversational Interfaces

As we contemplate the horizon of artificial intelligence, the anticipation of future developments in AI and conversational interfaces is not just a speculative exercise—it is a critical step towards preparing for a transformative leap in the way we interact with technology. The tapestry of AI is being woven with threads of advancement in computational power, algorithmic sophistication, and an expanding understanding of human language and sentiment.

The Emergence of Intuitive Interfaces

The conversational interfaces of the future promise to be more intuitive, capable of understanding and responding to a broader spectrum of human communication. As we progress, we foresee AI that can interpret intonation, emotional subtext, and cultural context—bridging the gap between human expression and machine interpretation. The prompt design, therefore, must evolve to facilitate this heightened level of interaction. The prompts of tomorrow will likely be less about instructing and more about conversing with AI, leveraging its deeper understanding to engage in more meaningful dialogue.

AI as Collaborative Partners

Looking ahead, we envisage AI not merely as tools or assistants but as collaborative partners. They will be integral in creative processes, problem-solving, and decision-making. This partnership will require prompts that are dynamic and adaptable, capable of guiding AI in its role as a contributor rather than merely a respondent. For example, in a brainstorming session, an AI might be prompted to suggest ideas and then evaluate their feasibility, fostering a collaborative environment where human creativity is augmented by AI's analytical prowess.

Ethical and Societal Considerations

As AI interfaces become more advanced, ethical, and societal considerations will come to the forefront. The design of AI prompts will need to account for ethical principles, ensuring that AI operates within the

Taha Baba

bounds of societal norms and values. This will involve crafting prompts that encourage AI to consider ethical implications and societal impact in its responses and actions.

Harnessing Emerging Technologies

Emerging technologies such as quantum computing and neuromorphic hardware will exponentially increase AI's capabilities. Anticipating these technologies, prompt design will need to harness this increased power to address more complex challenges, enabling AI to process and analyze data at speeds and depths previously unimaginable. The prompts will be the keys to unlocking these capabilities, directing AI's vast computational resources towards solving some of humanity's most pressing problems.

As we stand at the cusp of what AI might become, the importance of designing prompts that are ethically grounded, culturally aware, and technologically advanced becomes increasingly apparent. Our ability to anticipate the future of AI and conversational interfaces will shape the trajectory of our society's relationship with technology. The future beckons with a vision of AI that is seamlessly integrated into our lives, enhancing our capabilities, and enriching our experiences. It is a future that we are not just moving towards but one that we are actively shaping with every prompt we design today.

The Art of Prompt Perfection

As we close the pages of "The Art of Prompt Perfection: Mastering AI Conversations", we reflect on the journey through the intricate landscape of AI and conversational design. From the foundational elements of crafting effective prompts to the advanced strategies that harness AI's burgeoning capabilities, we have traversed a path that is as diverse as it is profound.

We began by charting the evolution of AI, understanding its history and the remarkable journey it has taken from simple rule-based systems to the complex neural networks of today. We explored the essence of conversational agents and their transformative impact on industries and daily life, underscoring the significance of precision in prompt design for optimizing AI interaction.

Through examples and case studies, we have illustrated the potential of AI in practical applications, from enhancing business solutions and educational experiences to enriching personal life and leisure. We delved into the importance of cultural and linguistic diversity in prompt design, recognizing the need for AI to communicate across the vast tapestry of human experience.

Looking to the future, we anticipated the impact of emerging technologies on AI and the role of interpretability in crafting prompts that foster trust and understanding. We envisioned next-generation conversational agents, equipped with cognitive empathy and cultural intelligence, ready to serve as collaborative partners in a myriad of human endeavours.

Yet, as we embrace these advancements, we must also remain vigilant of the ethical implications that accompany the integration of AI into the fabric of society. We have a collective responsibility to ensure that as AI continues to evolve, it does so with a commitment to ethical principles, inclusivity, and the betterment of humanity.

Taha Baba

The art of prompt perfection is not a static discipline but an ever-evolving craft that requires continuous learning, adaptation, and foresight. It is a dialogue between human creativity and machine intelligence, a symphony of human directives and AI responses that, together, create a harmonious interaction.

In this book, we have not only provided a roadmap for mastering AI conversations, but also ignited a conversation about the future of AI itself. As you, the reader, apply these insights, remember that every prompt is a building block in the edifice of AI's future—a future that we are shaping with every question, directive, and creative challenge we pose to the AI systems that are becoming an intrinsic part of our world.

Let us move forward with the knowledge that the art of prompt perfection is not just about the technology we create, but too about the human experiences we enhance through it. May we all continue to craft prompts that not only command but also inspire, guiding AI to its fullest potential while upholding the values we cherish as a society.

Taha Baba

References

1. "Neural Machine Translation by Jointly Learning and Aligning Source and Target Embeddings" by Vaswani et al. (2017): https://arxiv.org/abs/1609.08144

2. "Attention Is All You Need" by Vaswani et al. (2017): https://arxiv.org/abs/1706.03762

3. "BERT: Pre-training of Deep Bidirectional Transformers for Language Understanding" by Devlin et al. (2018): https://arxiv.org/abs/1810.04805

4. "Generative Pre-trained Transformer 3 (GPT-3)" by Brown et al. (2020): https://arxiv.org/abs/2005.14165

5. Hugging Face: https://huggingface.co/

6. TensorFlow Transformer Model Documentation: https://www.tensorflow.org/text/tutorials/transformer

7. "Case Study: Zara's Comprehensive Approach to AI and Supply Chain Management" by AIX (2023): https://aiexpert.network/case-study-zaras-comprehensive-approach-to-ai-and-supply-chain-management/

8. "How the Zara Supply Chain Taps into Top Clothing, Retail Trends" by Thomasnet (2023): https://www.thomasnet.com/insights/zara-supply-chain/

9. "Fashion at the Speed of Light: Delving into Zara Supply Chain Strategy" by DFreight (2023): https://dfreight.org/blog/delving-into-zara-supply-chain-strategy/

10. "How Zara Uses AI to Stay Ahead of the Fashion Curve" by Forbes (2022): https://www.forbes.com/sites/bernardmarr/2018/08/10/how-fashion-retailer-hm-is-betting-on-artificial-intelligence-and-big-data-to-regain-profitability/

11. "Zara's Just-In-telligent Supply Chain" by LinkedIn (2022): https://www.linkedin.com/pulse/zaras-just-in-telligent-supply-chain-sanish-mathews/

12. "Walmart's AI Saves $2 Billion by Predicting How Fast Lettuce Wilts" by The Wall Street Journal (2023)

13. "How AI is Reducing Food Waste at Major Retailers" by Forbes (2023)

14. "The Food Waste Reduction Roadmap: Driving Change in the Retail Industry" by The Food and Agriculture Organization (FAO) (2023)

15. "AI in Retail 2024: Trends, Applications, and Impact" by McKinsey & Company (2024)

16. Walmart Sustainability Report

17. Eden Sustainability Solutions Website

18. World Wildlife Fund (WWF) Food Waste Initiative: https://www.worldwildlife.org/initiatives/food-waste

19. International Journal of Retail & Distribution Management (2023)

Taha Baba

20. Podcast interview with Sal Khan, the founder and CEO of Khan Academy: https://www.cbsnews.com/news/khan-academy-founder-sal-kahn-on-filling-the-gaps-in-covid-impacted-education/

21. Article about Khan Academy's expansion into early learning and peer-to-peer tutoring: https://www.edsurge.com/news/2021-04-26-sal-khan-on-expanding-into-early-learning-and-launching-a-peer-to-peer-tutoring-platform

22. Article featuring Sal Khan's advice on education during COVID-19: https://www.cnet.com/tech/computing/sal-khan-how-to-help-students-and-parents-navigate-education-during-covid-19/

23. Google.org support for Khan Academy: https://www.google.org/covid-19/

24. Case study on Khan Academy using Zendesk: https://yourstory.com/2021/03/khan-academy-zendesk-remote-learners

25. Blog post reviewing the 7 best AI scheduling assistants in 2023: https://zapier.com/blog/best-ai-scheduling/

26. Article listing the 15 best AI scheduling assistants in 2024: https://ayanza.com/blog/ai-scheduling-assistants

27. Article comparing 10 best AI calendars in 2024: https://clickup.com/blog/ai-calendars/

28. Clara: https://www.aiclara.com

29. Trevor: https://www.aiclara.com/

30. AI scenario simulation using AI for training and evaluation: https://www.zenarate.com/blog/ai-conversation-simulation/

31. AI scenario simulation for customer service and emergency preparedness and response: https://www.forbes.com/sites/forbesbusinesscouncil/2022/04/21/how-to-improve-contact-center-training-with-ai-simulation/

Taha Baba

Printed in Great Britain
by Amazon

38503451R00046